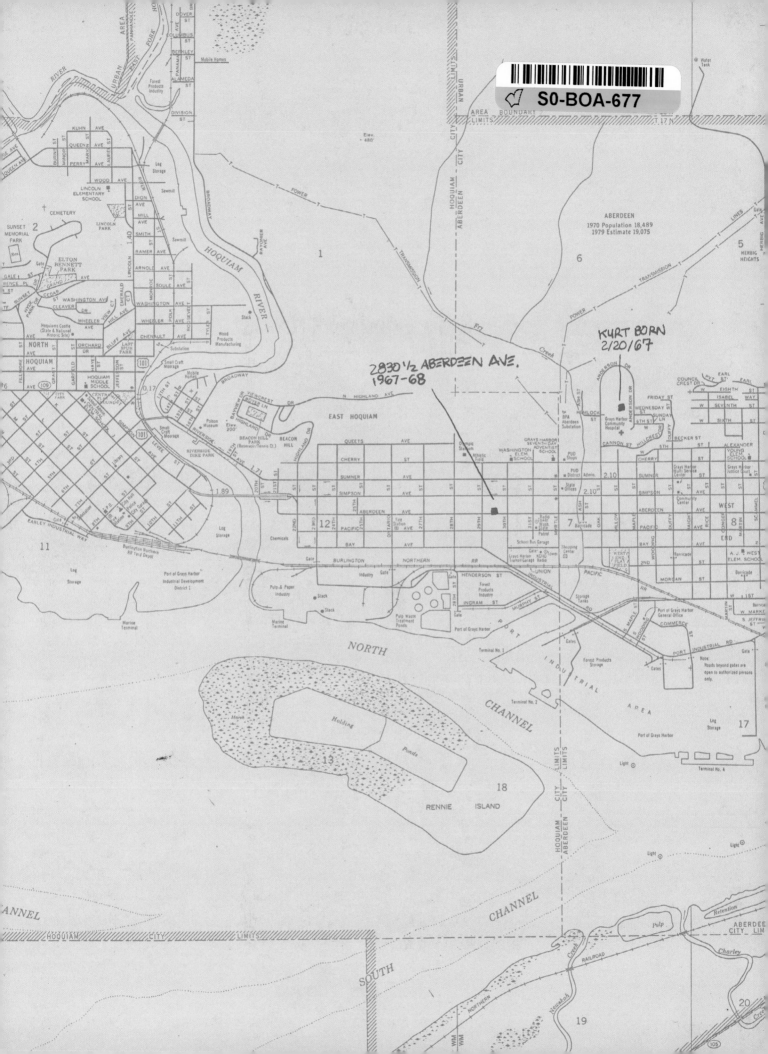

S0-BOA-677

COVER During the six years of his professional career, thousands of photos were taken of Kurt Cobain both in concert and offstage—but he hated the bulk of them. This photograph, taken at Seattle's legendary Crocodile Cafe in the fall of 1992, was one of the few personal snapshots Kurt liked enough to keep in his own scrapbook.

PREVIOUS This picture of Kurt playing guitar sat in a small locket-type frame on a nightstand next to Kurt and Courtney's bed. Courtney cites it as one of her favorite pictures because she loved the shape and beauty of Kurt's hands.

ALSO BY CHARLES R. CROSS

BACKSTREETS: SPRINGSTEEN, THE MAN AND HIS MUSIC

LED ZEPPELIN: HEAVEN AND HELL

NEVERMIND: THE CLASSIC ALBUM

HEAVIER THAN HEAVEN: A BIOGRAPHY OF KURT COBAIN

ROOM FULL OF MIRRORS: A BIOGRAPHY OF JIMI HENDRIX

COBAIN UNSEEN

CHARLES R. CROSS

LITTLE, BROWN AND COMPANY

NEW YORK   BOSTON   LONDON

Copyright © 2008 by The End of Music, LLC

Text copyright © 2008 by Charles R. Cross

All rights reserved. Except as permitted under the U.S. Copyright Act of 1976, no part of this
publication may be reproduced, distributed, or transmitted in any form or by any means, or
stored in a database or retrieval system, without the prior written permission of the publisher.

Little, Brown and Company
Hachette Book Group USA
237 Park Avenue, New York, NY 10017
Visit our Web site at www.HachetteBookGroupUSA.com

First Edition: October 2008

Little, Brown and Company is a division of Hachette Book Group USA, Inc.
The Little, Brown name and logo are trademarks of Hachette Book Group USA, Inc.

Library of Congress Cataloging-in-Publication Data
Cross, Charles R.
  Cobain unseen / Charles R. Cross. — 1st ed.
     p. cm.
  ISBN-13: 978-0-316-03372-5
  ISBN-10: 0-316-03372-3
  1. Cobain, Kurt, 1967-1994. 2. Rock musicians — United States — Biography. I. Title.
  ML420.C59C75 2008
  782.42166092 — dc22
  [B]   2008014164

CREATIVE CONSULTANT, RESEARCHER, AND ARCHIVIST Ava Stander
DESIGNER Joanna Price
EDITOR Meghan Cleary
PHOTO RESEARCHER Shayna Ian
PRODUCTION COORDINATOR Leah Finger

10 9 8 7 6 5 4 3 2 1

Printed in China

PROLOGUE THE SECRET MUSEUM

"I feel this society has somewhere lost its sense of what art is. Art is expression. In expression you need 100 percent full freedom, and our freedom to express our art is seriously being fucked with."
—AN ENTRY IN ONE OF KURT COBAIN'S JOURNALS

THE DOOR WAS ALREADY OPEN, so I knocked on the frame. For a long time, no one appeared, and I was left staring into a tiny Olympia, Washington, apartment and pondering its mystery and history. As with most things you imagine before you see them, the place was smaller than I had expected. My mind had given it a scale based on the significance of what happened here, rather than the simple fact that it was a one-bedroom apartment that in 1989 rented for $137.50 a month. Finally, a twenty-something college student wearing boxer shorts appeared on the threshold. I'm certain he initially thought I was selling magazines or saving souls. When I flashed the badges of my profession—tape recorder, notebook, and camera—he shrugged his shoulders and invited my companion and me in, pointing toward a saggy sofa behind a flea-market coffee table.

Biographers are sometimes forced by necessity to be nosy, and such was the case on this day in the spring of 1999 when I found myself asking to tour this man's home. He was nice about it and told me I could have the run of the place. It was tiny, and I walked the entire apartment in sixty seconds.

Mostly, it was what I had anticipated: a typical apartment in a run-down house. I'd already seen a floor plan, so I knew where the infamous bedroom wall was—once covered with "Kurt smells like Teen Spirit" graffiti—and I knew that there were two other apartments in the house. Yet floor plans hadn't captured the smell, which was equal parts pet-shop muskiness, cheap-ramen-noodle infusion, and the essence of one-too-many burned pots of Kraft macaroni and cheese.

It was in this apartment that Kurt Cobain crafted his unlikely musical revolution. He sat down one day in this tiny place and wrote out the first draft of "Smells Like Teen Spirit," not even knowing the name referred to a deodorant. In doing so, he forever recast the parameters of what the chorus of a pop anthem might include ("An albino, a mosquito, my libido"). At the same time, he expanded the emotional landscape of rock music: Anger, alienation, and angst were added to the canon. From this diminutive place, he created, with Nirvana, a broad musical vision that forever changed popular music.

RIGHT A two-year-old Kurt at his aunt Mari's home, holding a tambourine. He loved music even from an early age, and was exposed to bands like the Byrds (pictured on the three posters behind him) by his aunts and uncles.

FOLLOWING Kurt collected toys and games that he bought at thrift stores, garage sales, and hobby shops. The only unifying theme in his collections is that everything reflected the oddity of American pop culture in some twisted way. Often, he customized these collectibles by painting over them or distorting their appearance. Kurt doctored this Freddy Krueger figurine, issued sometime around the 1984 release of *Nightmare on Elm Street*, to include a twine noose. The artifact hung for a time, literally, on the wall of his Olympia apartment.

The apartment didn't look like much, but it was all Kurt could afford at the time, and he could barely manage to pay the rent. Here he wrote songs, watched countless hours of television, ate gelatinous cheese products, wrote hundreds of entries in his journals, painted dozens of pieces of art, and suffered, as he suffered nearly everywhere. Sitting in the sordid flat, I could imagine the frustration he must have felt with his circumstances, particularly during the years when his band couldn't get a label deal. One of the greatest myths in rock history is that Nirvana was an overnight success. In truth, the band did nine tours and played together for four years before they became successful; during most of that time of struggle, Kurt lived in abject poverty in this Olympia apartment. From this humble address, he dispatched hundreds of letters to record labels, begging them to sign him. He even offered to finance the release: "We are willing to *pay* for the majority of pressing of 1,000 copies of our LP, and all of the recording costs. . . ." he pleaded in one such missive. "*PLEASE* send us a reply of 'fuck off,' or, 'not interested,' so we don't have to waste more money sending more tapes." The postage alone was killing him.

The anomie Kurt felt during that period is easier to fathom than what happened four years later, at the height of his fame, when he took his own life in the greenhouse of his fifteen-room Seattle mansion. Every year, thousands of fans visit the park that abuts that mansion, but few have ever seen Kurt's one-time Olympia residence, in part because it is a private home and even meddlesome biographers are barely tolerated. Perhaps I was only let in because I visited it with Tracy Marander, who for a time had lived in the apartment with Kurt, back when they were dating. The current tenant may have had more sympathy for a former resident coming back to search for pieces of her past than he might have had for a reporter.

Tracy was kind enough to give me a tour that described what the place used to look like—there was once a Beatles poster on the wall and pictures of diseased vaginas on the refrigerator. The graffiti "Kurt smells like Teen Spirit" in the bedroom had gone up after Tracy and Kurt had split, and it had been painted over long ago. Kurt was

evicted from this apartment in 1991 for not paying his rent while he was in Los Angeles recording *Nevermind*, and the graffiti, along with many of his creations, was lost.

Yet sitting on a shelf out in the garage, there was still a concrete connection to Kurt's legacy. The garage was an unheated shack that made even the humble apartment look posh, and Kurt spent time there repairing the guitars and amps he smashed onstage. He also used the garage as a studio when he worked on art projects that required more space, as Tracy was pointing out when she peered up on a storage shelf. "That's Kurt's tent," she said. Technically, it was her tent, as during their time together she bought everything they owned. Like the debris of many a breakup, the tent had remained with the house, and Kurt used it on the occasional camping trip. It wasn't like the discovery of a lost guitar or a missing reel of tape, but it struck me as spooky nonetheless. Kurt had been dead five years at that point and hadn't lived in Olympia for almost a decade, but there, hidden in a cubbyhole, a part of him remained.

MOST OF THE EFFECTS that once filled that Olympia apartment and the other residences in Kurt Cobain's short life now sit in a secure high-tech storage facility hidden from sunlight and the eyes of fans. In researching my 2001 biography of Cobain, *Heavier Than Heaven*, I toured virtually every place Kurt ever rested his head, plus I had the great fortune to examine his personal effects that were in that storage space: his diaries, paintings, unreleased recordings, correspondence, home movies, record albums, and the ephemera in his collection of oddities. When I first saw many of these items, I was struck by how visual he was and how the music only told part of the story of Kurt's creativity and obsession. Even in the age before eBay, he was a fanatical collector of heart-shaped boxes, porcelain dolls, Visible Man models, and other curiosities. Haunting thrift stores and swap meets, he bought old View-Master slides, 1960s board games, plastic drink stirrers, action figure toys, and anomalous books and magazines. Considering that Kurt was homeless for part of his adulthood, I was shocked at how much of his stuff—how much of this odd collection—still survived.

On display in his various homes when he was alive, these spoils were in effect a traveling museum of American weirdness. Kurt's collectibles were mirrored by themes he wrote about in his journals and his music. "An albino, a mosquito" or, better yet, "With the lights out, it's less dangerous" made sense, in a warped way, to anyone who ever walked into his Olympia apartment and saw an Archie Bunker board game sitting next to an Evel Knievel action figure. "His whole house was cluttered, and there were things everywhere," Nirvana bassist Krist Novoselic once told me. "Yet he was a serious artist, and that was one of the ways he expressed himself—how he filtered the world. It came out a lot of ways, and some of it was morbid and twisted. In fact, all the art is decadent and twisted. His theme was pretty consistent: Everything was just a little fucked-up and dark."

This book is a private, pictorial peek into the twisted Kurt Cobain collection, a never-before-seen dark museum of fucked-up-ness. I've already written a biography of Kurt, so consider this an adjunct: a book focusing on his creative life, including a secret visual history of the things he created and collected. Pictured are many of the items you would have seen had you walked into that Olympia apartment in 1990 or visited the handful of other locales where Kurt lived in adulthood. You'll also find never-before-seen curios from his childhood, including intimate snapshots, rare Polaroids, and early Nirvana memorabilia. Unseen photographs, a few of them even taken by Kurt himself, will show you his world from his perspective.

Whether he was in the recording studio or in his apartment with an easel, Kurt did not consider himself an artist in the traditional sense. "An artist is in need of constant tragedy to fully express their work," he once wrote in his diary. "I'm not an artist." Later in the same entry, he lamented, "I feel this society has somewhere lost its sense of what art is." It was a divine paradox that made Kurt Cobain such a talent but also contributed to his many personal demons. Still, whether he would have classified himself as such or not, Kurt most certainly suffered the artist's predicament: The very reasons he felt pain were the fuel that drove his artistic passion. His dysfunction was his greatest gift and his heaviest burden.

If you had walked into that Olympia apartment when Kurt was in residence, you would have seen his abnormal world on display. On the walls were his drawings, posters he'd doctored by adding mustaches, and graffiti written directly on the wall with magic marker. And on the coffee table—probably the same beat-up wood coffee table I rested my feet on when I visited in 1999—you'd have seen his journals sitting next to a Mr. T action figure. He did not hide his stuff, not even his journals, but instead felt great pride in showing them off. Many of Kurt's friends reported that when they visited, he shared cartoons or passages from his journals, and he enjoyed having an audience for his creative work. Now you are part of that intimate audience.

One page of those journals offers a contradictory view on whether Kurt wanted these creations to be private after his death: "Don't read my diary when I'm gone," he wrote at the top of a lined sheet of paper. And then, as if he'd rethought that idea as soon as he had written it, he backtracked. "Please read my diary," he pleaded. He most likely wrote these words in 1990, four years before his death and a year before the apex of his fame. Nonetheless, they read like a self-penned epitaph: "Look through my things," his scrawled penmanship asks, "and figure me out." ∎

1

BURNING HIPPIES

Kurt Cobain was born on February 20, 1967, at Grays Harbor Community Hospital in Aberdeen, Washington. Kurt, in his typical fashion, later wrote in one of his many self-penned biographies that he was born in "the year they burned the hippie." With no small level of regret, he noted that his parents were not from the counterculture. "The closest thing my parents came to a hippie," Kurt wrote, "was our VW van, which my dad painted like a ladybug."

His mother, Wendy, was only nineteen when Kurt was born, and his father, Don, was just twenty-one. Don worked as a mechanic at a Chevron gas station, a job he was happy to have in an era where Aberdeen's unemployment rate was the highest in Washington. Few, if any, rock stars have been born into such hardship. The Cobains' rental house was little more than a shack in an alley behind another real house. Their residence was so tiny and decrepit, it made even Elvis Presley's birthplace in Tupelo, Mississippi, look palatial by contrast. Only when Don got a $5-a-month raise were they able to afford a larger, if equally modest, house down the street. Kurt was the couple's first child, followed three years later by his sister, Kimberly.

In his journals Kurt wrote several contradictory versions of his early childhood. One story, written when he was twenty-four, reads: "I was born a white, lower-middle-class male off the coast of Washington State. My parents owned a compact stereo component system molded in simulated wood grain and a four-record box set featuring AM radio's contemporary hits of the early seventies called *Good Vibrations* by Ronco. It had such hits as Tony Orlando and Dawn's 'Tie a Yellow Ribbon' and Jim Croce's 'Time in a Bottle.' After years of my begging, they finally bought me a tin drum set with paper heads out of the back of a Sears catalog." In other diary entries, he painted his parents as less giving, and his "begging" was played up.

The drum became Kurt's first foray into music and his first demonstration of any kind of creative gift. Even as a baby, he beat on it like a junior Ringo Starr. Neighbors recalled him pounding on the drum in the yard as soon as he could walk, looking like the leader of a marching band. A few

RIGHT A portrait of the young man as an artist. For his eighth birthday in February 1975, Kurt received this easel from his paternal grandparents. Comic book characters were his favorite art subjects in childhood; he began with Disney-related fare, such as Donald Duck, but quickly moved to superheroes. Here, Kurt is copying the cover from *Giant-Size Werewolf* #4, an April 1975 Marvel comic.

BELOW Clockwise from top left: Kurt at five months old with his father, Don, July 1967 (a note on the back of the photograph reads "Kurt's first time to steer the car"); Kurt holds a pipe on his first birthday in February 1968; Kurt on his second birthday in February 1969 with his maternal grandfather; Kurt models his "Little Lord Fauntleroy" outfit at one of his uncles' houses, Christmas 1968. The dates on most of Kurt's childhood photos reflect a two-month time lag; finding extra money to pay for film developing was a strain on the family's finances.

Immunization Record

NAME _Kurt Cobain_

BIRTHDAY _Feb. 20 - 1967_

J. D. Ehrhart M. D.
PHYSICIAN'S SIGNATURE

IMMUNIZATIONS		Date of First Course	Date of Booster	Next Immunization Due
Diphtheria Tetanus (Lockjaw) Pertussis (Whooping Cough) }	**TRI-IMMUNOL*** *TRADE-MARK Vaccine	5-23-67 7-11-67 8-15-67		1 month HAD IT 5 years
Smallpox (Vaccination)		10/7/67		10/10/72
Typhoid-Paratyphoid Fever				
Measles (Poliomyelitis Immune Globulin [Human]) Live vaccine		3/24/70		—
Mumps				
Poliomyelitis Vaccine (Sabin)		5-23-67		
		7-11-67		
		3-8-68		
Tri measles —		3/24/70		

ABOVE The front and inside of Kurt's infant immunization card.

RIGHT Don Cobain holding one-week-old baby Kurt, whose hair was dark when he was first born but quickly became blond.

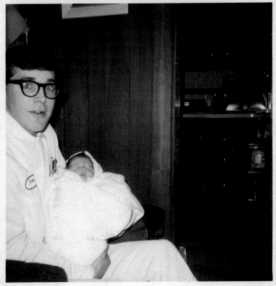

APR • 67

TOP LEFT Just two days after Kurt's eighth birthday, on February 22, 1975, Kurt is pictured reading a book to his sister, who was home ill.

BOTTOM LEFT For Christmas in 1974, Kurt got his precious drum set, and Kim received a baby buggy.

TOP RIGHT Kurt's copy of his aunt Mari's 1985 single, on which she wrote, "To Kurt: You're so special! Love You! Love, Aunt Mari." Mari's career as a musician and her constant encouragement of Kurt had a great influence on him.

ENCLOSURE Kurt drew this Thanksgiving-themed card for his father, stepmother, and family. He was already self-aware enough to write "A Kurt Cobain Greeting Card" on the back.

years later, he got a real drum set for Christmas, and he also whaled away on that. Though his early attempts at playing the drum did not strike anyone as showing musical virtuosity, he did have a very strong interest in making music.

Several of Kurt's aunts and uncles were musicians, and he grew up in a world where music was part of the family landscape. One of his uncles had a band that played around the region, and his aunt Mari made a living as a singer/songwriter. Kurt's mother came from a large German family, and sing-alongs were part of any holiday or birthday gathering. Kurt was always in the center of these sing-alongs, and if not singing, he was at least enjoying the idea of a house where music was welcomed.

Kurt's aunt Mari, in particular, had an indelible effect on him when she gave him her old albums. Throughout his adult life, Kurt cited this generosity as a turning point in his interest in rock. "She's definitely the most helpful person in my life as far as music," he told Michael Azerrad for the authorized biography *Come as You Are*. "She gave me an electric Hawaiian guitar and amplifier when I was like eight years old. And she was the one responsible for giving me the Beatles records." Kurt recalled how he'd strap on his bass drum "and an Elmer Fudd hat, and my dad's tennis shoes, and walk around the neighborhood singing Beatle songs."

When Kurt was two, his parents bought their first house, a modest two-story home in a lower-middle-class neighborhood. Later, they acquired a piano, and though Kurt never took lessons, he experimented with this instrument. "He could sit down and just play something he'd heard on the radio," recalled his sister, Kim. "He was able to artistically put whatever he thought onto paper or into music."

By all accounts Kurt was a creative child, but once he could easily hold a crayon or pencil in his hand, music became secondary to drawing. Like most toddlers, he was given markers and paper to entertain himself, and he could spend hours so occupied. His interest in drawing was significant enough that his parents imagined he might have a career that involved art. "It was my mom's big dream," his sister remembered, "that Kurt and I would end up at Disneyland, both of us working there, with him drawing." Kurt confirmed this in a 1991 interview with Roy Trakin: "My mother encouraged me a lot to be artistic. It was written in a contract at an early age that I would be an artist."

When anyone in Kurt's extended family had a birthday or celebration, Kurt would draw a greeting card as a gift. Many copies of his childhood art still exist, kept by his relatives because they expressed both a sweet sentiment and budding artistic promise. For his paternal grandfather, Leland Cobain, Kurt once drew a card with a picture of Donald Duck. It was so accurate that Leland accused Kurt of tracing it; to prove him wrong, Kurt drew it again. Kurt excelled at Disney characters and comic book superheroes. Tony Hirschman was in Kurt's kindergarten class and observed that he showed exceptional skill, even at that premature an age: "He was an amazing artist. That guy could draw anything. Once we were looking at pictures of werewolves, and he drew one that looked just like the photo."

One of Kurt's relatives had a birthday near Thanksgiving, and in 1980, Kurt drew a card for his family that showed an impish-looking little pilgrim holding a turkey leg in his hand. Kurt was only thirteen at the time, but here were already touches that spoke to the unique sense of humor he'd display as an adult: The inside of the paper read "Burp," next to the pilgrim was a martini glass, and on the back of the card he had written, "A Kurt Cobain Greeting Card," with a trademark symbol next to it.

When he was in second grade, Kurt's artwork was selected to be on the cover of the elementary school newspaper. At school or at home, he was constantly drawing, and he put many of his art projects up on his bedroom walls. Soon the bedroom became a gallery of crayon creations.

At an early age, Kurt also showed interest in multidimensional projects. He experimented with modeling putty and clay, making crude sculptures of aliens or superheroes. When he visited his paternal grandparents, whose taste in art was more traditional, his muse was piqued in another direction. His grandmother Iris loved Norman Rockwell, and Kurt often helped her re-create famous Rockwell paintings by etching them onto dried mushrooms with toothpicks. With his grandfather Leland, Kurt learned to use a table saw and helped build a dollhouse for Iris. "Kurt helped me shingle it," Leland recalled. "It took twelve hours to shingle it, and Kurt did a lot of it."

As early as second grade, Kurt was already having trouble sitting still in class. Other times, as when he worked on the dollhouse, he had the opposite problem of becoming so engrossed in one project that he ignored all else. At seven, Kurt was given Ritalin to control his hyperactivity and attention deficit. In his adult life, Kurt frequently cited his early medication as one of the reasons he later became a drug addict. He wasn't aware of the fact that some research studies support his claim in suggesting that children who are heavily medicated are more likely to abuse drugs as adults. The hyperactivity drugs didn't particularly help Kurt, and his parents eventually took him off the medication, though he later said that he felt the damage had already been done.

INTERNALLY, THE YOUNG KURT FELT DIFFERENT FROM OTHER CHILDREN, or so he later wrote in his journal. Most of those who grew up around him felt, in retrospect, that Kurt suffered from depression, though he was never treated or medicated for the condition in his youth. His family physician had prescribed the Ritalin to deal with Kurt's level of frantic activity, not anticipating the inevitable lows that followed.

RIGHT A nine-year-old Kurt lifts up a volcanic rock on a family vacation in 1976.

INSIDE FLAP One of Kurt's early watercolor paintings, done when he was ten years old.

OUTSIDE FLAP Another watercolor, painted at age thirteen.

Mental health problems, including depression and addiction, ran in his family on both sides, and several of his relatives had attempted suicide or died from it. His maternal great-grandfather had attempted suicide by stabbing himself in front of his family; that man later died from his wounds in the same hospital that once held Kurt's idol Frances Farmer. On Kurt's paternal side, one great-uncle drank himself to an early death, while two others committed suicide by gunshot. One of those uncles shot himself in the head; this particularly grisly death was a frequent source of sarcastic comedy for the teenaged Kurt, who was fond of telling his friends that this uncle had "killed himself over the death of Jim Morrison."

When Kurt was nine, his parents divorced. Almost twenty years later, as late as 1993, he was still writing about the event in his journal and in songs like "Serve the Servants." In that song, off *In Utero*, he sings, "That legendary divorce / is such a bore." The very fact that it remained "legendary," and was often talked about by Kurt in interviews, suggests it was anything but a "bore" and continued as a pressing issue in Kurt's life. Along with his childhood use of Ritalin, Kurt forever linked the divorce with his many problems.

Despite the fact that Kurt frequently cited "the age of eight" as the point when he became "hateful to all humans," most observers don't date his problems back that far. At first, the divorce actually improved Kurt's emotional circumstances, as he moved in with his father and the fighting between his parents lessened with their separation. Though Kurt and Don lived in a tiny single-wide trailer and remained incredibly poor, the male bonding seemed to serve Kurt well, and neither his grades nor his friendships initially suffered. "I moved in with my dad into a trailer park in an even smaller logging community," he wrote in his journal. "My dad's friends talked him into joining the Columbia Record Club and soon records showed up at my trailer almost once a week."

Even when Don remarried, Kurt seemed to thrive at first, and the addition of a stepbrother and stepsister made him feel like a part of a larger, more legitimate, family. The remarriage also meant a move to Montesano, a small town eight miles east of Aberdeen. "Monte," as the locals call it, was more close-knit, and Kurt found it easy to make new friends.

In junior high, Kurt was considered something of a preppy by schoolmates, and he was well liked. His class photos show a handsome teen wearing striped polo shirts. He tried out for football, wrestling, and track, but only stuck with wrestling. "It was no exaggeration to say that he was one of the most popular kids," observed classmate Roni Toyra. "He was a bit of a show-off. There were kids who were unhappy, or who were outcasts, but he wasn't one of them."

WHEN KURT WAS IN EIGHTH GRADE, an event occurred that had as much significance as the divorce, in the way it left an impression on his young mind. Kurt walked to school every day, a trip of less than a

ABOVE Kurt, his stepbrother, and his stepsister on a family vacation at Sun Lakes Park Resort, near eastern Washington's Coulee City, in the late seventies.

ABOVE RIGHT Kurt, his mother, and his sister on a Puget Sound ferry around 1980.

mile. One morning, he and two friends took a shortcut through the woods and came upon the body of a young man who had hung himself from a tree the night before. It was the brother of a friend, so Kurt knew the victim. Furthermore, the corpse was hanging at a bizarre angle, with twisted limbs adding to the gruesomeness. Kurt stood around and watched the body twist in the wind for almost an hour as rescue workers descended upon the scene. "I remember the principal running across the parking lot with a butter knife to try to cut the kid down," recalled Rod Marsh, who also witnessed it. "It was the most grotesque thing I ever saw in my life." It was only after Kurt had observed for quite some time that an adult finally shooed him away, thinking that maybe this ghoulish visage was not one a young man should have witnessed. But the damage was already done; Kurt talked about the suicide obsessively, and it became one of the defining moments in his young life.

Though Kurt had a typical teenage sense of humor that was already cynical, coming upon the dead body seemed to give his quips an even more morbid tone. Walking home from school one day with his friend John Fields, Kurt made a prediction that later would seem eerily prescient: "I'm going to be a superstar musician, kill myself, and go out in a flame of glory," he boasted. Fields told Kurt not to talk about dying. "I want to be rich and famous and kill myself like Jimi Hendrix," Kurt replied. (At the time, Kurt was under the mistaken impression that Hendrix had died from suicide.) Fields was not the only friend of Kurt's who heard such macabre talk. "He told me he had suicide genes," recalled Rod Marsh. "I didn't know what to think of that. We were only in the seventh grade."

KURT'S FASCINATION WITH EARLY DEATH fueled his artistic muse. Around the time he began junior high, he started to experiment with filmmaking, using his father's Super 8 movie camera. He began by creating stop-action Claymation adventures that owed much to the work of Will Vinton. Later, he wrote elaborate plots for these productions, one of which showed aliens landing in the backyard. Kurt had always been fascinated with the idea of aliens, and while other teenage boys drew cars or tanks in their notebooks, he sketched extraterrestrial beings or zombies.

One film, made in 1982 when Kurt was fifteen, owed more to Wes Craven than to Ray Bradbury. He titled it *Kurt Commits Bloody Suicide*. While his stepbrother held the camera, Kurt used a serrated aluminum can to pretend to cut his wrists. As the camera panned on him, Kurt shrieked in agony, while leaking gallons of red Kool-Aid from his wounds. He fell to the ground and "died," overacting the death scene like a vaudevillian ham. In another film, made around the same time, Kurt cut his own throat with a fake knife and again acted out his final moments. The slasher theme was common in these crude films, and Kurt often played a vigilante, stalking victims with guns, knives, or baseball bats, mocking moves he'd seen in horror films.

Suicide was an often-covered topic in Kurt's journals, sometimes talked about in a worldly context ("our generation is subconsciously committing suicide"), and sometimes discussed in more personal detail. Around the time he discovered the dead man in the tree, Kurt had what he later described as his "first sexual encounter" with another person, an event that nearly drove him to suicide, and an event that, tellingly, had transpired as a direct result of Kurt's early contemplations of taking his own life.

A friend of Kurt's had a developmentally disabled sister. In Kurt's own varied tellings of the story, she suffered from Down syndrome, was "half-retarded," or was only "slightly disabled." Kurt and two friends went to the girl's house after school to raid her parents' liquor cabinet. His friends left, and the girl undressed before him. They engaged in foreplay and attempted sexual intercourse. "I tried to fuck her, but I didn't know how," he wrote in his journal. He asked her if she had ever had sex before, and she replied, "A lot of times," mainly "with her cousin." Though Kurt was disgusted by this incest-implying revelation, the confession did not deter him, and he attempted intercourse again. Ultimately, he became repulsed by the way she smelled, so he ended the event prematurely and left. Kurt was always obsessed with smell and odor, and his highly attuned olfactory sense was forever linked with sexuality to an abnormal degree.

As described in Kurt's journal, the tale then became one of crime and punishment. Kurt wrote that he was so filled with remorse, he stayed out of school for the next week, and when he did return, he was given "in-house suspension." He also claimed the girl's father went to the school and accused Kurt of rape, and Kurt was then taken to the Montesano police station and questioned. No record

LEFT Even as a child, Kurt wore his hair long for the era in a shag-style cut. On the top he's pictured with his sister, Kim, while the bottom two photos are official school shots from elementary and junior high.

of any such police investigation exists, nor do Kurt's friends recall the matter being this serious, so these details were likely a creation of Kurt's overactive imagination. In Kurt's telling of the event, he only escaped prosecution by a rare stroke of luck: The girl was shown a school yearbook and asked to identify her attacker. She failed to find her abuser, according to Kurt's journal entry, because he had been absent on photo day. In truth, Kurt is pictured in all his junior high school yearbooks, so this element is again most likely a further embellishment. In another version of the story, Kurt wrote that he only escaped prosecution because "she was eighteen and *not* mentally retarded," contradicting what he had said elsewhere. Again, this account is based on Kurt's varied tellings, which are not to be taken for the truth.

His childhood friends do confirm that there was an incident between Kurt and a girl, and that he felt shame about it. What is most significant about the event is that Kurt wrote that he had only undertaken the sexual adventure because earlier that week he had contemplated suicide and decided he needed to have sex before dying. "That month happened to be the epitome of my mental abuse from my mother," he wrote. "I decided that within the next month, I'll not sit on my roof and *think* about jumping but I'll *actually* kill myself." The story is also significant because it illustrates the unhealthy connection that Kurt made between sexuality and inner shame. Though most adolescent boys suffer from questions about their own blossoming interest in sex, that Kurt's imagination included such bizarre and fantastic turmoil demonstrates pathology beyond the normal.

Wanting to jump off the roof may have been the first time Kurt seriously considered taking his own life, but it was by no means the last. Even during his youth, he talked about dying often and was convinced he would not live long. When Kurt later came seemingly out of nowhere to become famous, many of his childhood friends were less surprised by his success than they were by the fact that he'd survived adolescence, considering how frequently he talked about death.

By eighth grade, suicide was even beginning to show up as a theme in some of the nascent songs Kurt was writing. When another classmate, named Beau, took his own life, Kurt composed a song, titled "Ode to Beau," about the boy. He wrote it in the style of a country-and-western crooner, and it sounded not unlike the maudlin "Seasons in the Sun," about a dying man—that 1974 hit by Terry Jacks about a premature death also happened to be the first record that Kurt Cobain ever bought. ∎

2

AMERICAN GOTHIC

n February 1980, Kurt turned fourteen and a birthday present changed his life: a six-string Lindell electric guitar. Though it took him time to become proficient at the instrument, the guitar would become his single greatest creative outlet over the course of his life. He played it for hours, and few things consistently gave him as much joy.

Though Kurt later implied that he picked up the guitar and started right in with classic punk rock anthems, his initial musical interest mirrored that of most other boys his age: garage rock and heavy metal. The first song he learned to play from start to finish was "Louie Louie," which had been a regional hit by both the Kingsmen and the Fabulous Wailers in the Northwest two decades before. After starting with garage rock, Kurt moved on to heavy metal. His guitar teacher reported that the song Kurt most wanted to play was "Stairway to Heaven." His instructor taught Kurt basic Zeppelin chords and AC/DC chops over a span of several months.

The guitar, however, was not simply a creative outlet for Kurt; it became a fashion accessory. He carried it with him everywhere, if only to let people know he was now a guitarist. When the cheap instrument broke and was unplayable, he still took it with him. "I saw Kurt with it on the street," recalled his friend Trevor Briggs. "He told me, 'Don't ask me to play any songs on this; it's broken.'"

Kurt had always been interested in music, but owning a guitar accelerated that fascination. He subscribed to *Creem* magazine and regularly read *The Rocket*, the regional music magazine that cost a quarter at the only store in Aberdeen that carried it. And though he later went out of his way to suggest that this was a time when he enjoyed only punk rock, his own journals tell a very different story: AC/DC, Led Zeppelin, Judas Priest, Iron Maiden, and Black Sabbath were the band logos he scribbled in his notebooks when he was supposed to be doing homework.

One of Kurt's most characteristic pieces of revisionist history came after he became famous—he told reporters that the first rock concert he'd ever seen was Black Flag at a Seattle club. In truth, his first show was the more pedestrian pairing of Sammy Hagar and Quarterflash at the Seattle

RIGHT By high school, Kurt's personal style—and artistic subjects—had shifted dramatically. He drew these senior-citizen punk rockers (an offbeat tribute to Grant Wood's *American Gothic*) in pencil, then used an airbrush to color the background. Someone who liked the image purchased it for a few dollars at a high school art show; later the drawing was sold to the Experience Music Project museum in Seattle. It has never been displayed.

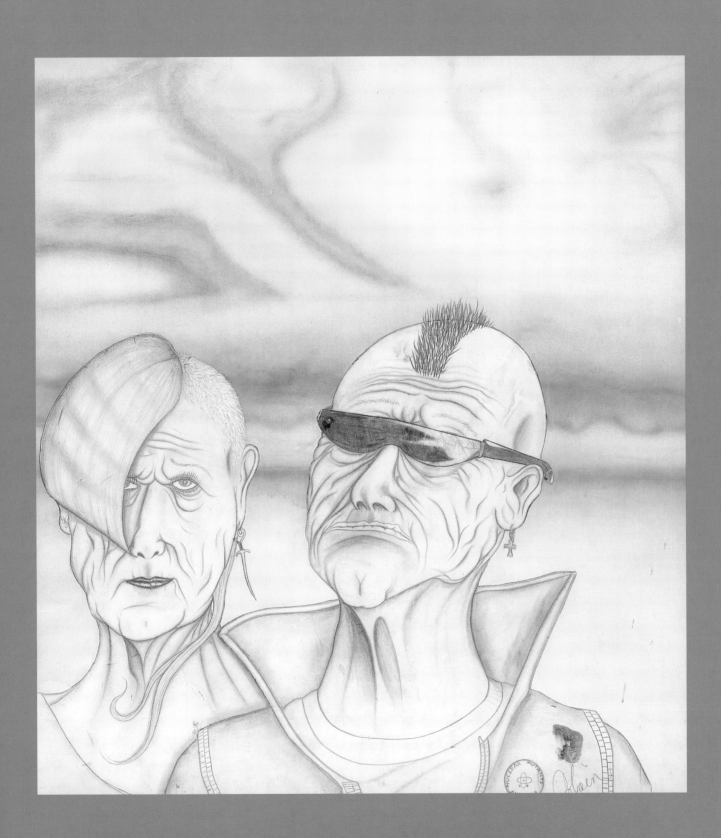

Center Coliseum in 1983. The next day at school, he proudly wore the Sammy Hagar T-shirt he'd purchased the night before.

THE SAMMY HAGAR CONCERT was one of Kurt's few pleasures that year. His home life had become more troubled, as conflicts with his father and stepmother grew until fights became a daily occurrence; on weekends, when he visited his mother in Aberdeen, he fought with her as well. This was beyond normal teenage/parent conflict, and it escalated to the degree that they decided to send Kurt to live with other relatives. First he stayed with one uncle and later was shifted to another. A few months after this series of moves, he was back with his mother in Aberdeen. Having four addresses in less than a year wreaked havoc on Kurt's academic life. Up until that point, he'd gotten decent grades, and most remembered him as a bright student, but by tenth grade he was close to flunking out. His decreasing grades had a negative effect on his self-esteem, and drawing and music became his only refuges.

His problems with school and parents were exacerbated by his drug use, though Kurt later embellished and exaggerated these stories, like many from this period. He experimented with marijuana, LSD, and several other drugs when he could find and afford them, but rarely could he do either. Aberdeen was not awash in drugs during that decade, and alcohol was the substance most abused by local teenagers. Anytime Kurt could find booze, he drank it, seeking to block out the emotional emptiness he felt inside.

ABOVE No matter how ratty and shrunken Kurt's well-worn T-shirts might have become, he kept them. A handful of the collection pictured above—including "Cheap Trick Tour 1980" (far left) and "Aberdeen Historical Whorehouse Restoration Society" (fourth from left)—date from Kurt's teen years in Aberdeen.

His move back to Aberdeen was fraught with troubles as well, and he clashed with his mother frequently. Part of the problem may have been his untreated depression. "I now know, in hindsight, that the sleeping he was doing in his teenage years was the very beginning of it," his mother later told *Entertainment Weekly*. "That was also masked by just being a teenager. But now I look back and go, 'Aha, that was the very beginning of it.'"

His room became his one sanctuary, and he rarely left it, often sleeping in and missing school. In this one private space, he drew, listened to albums, and played his guitar. He took down many of his own drawings and covered the walls of the room with concert posters and flyers—it was the beginning of a curating fetish he'd embrace fully later in his life.

As for the conflicts with adults, Kurt blamed his mother, Wendy, for many of his problems. In one of the frequent journal entries in which he wrote about his self-described "worthless" adolescence, he described this period as "total depression, total hatred, and grudges that would last months at a time." He hated Wendy's boyfriends and hated that his friends thought his mother was "hot" and told him so. One of Wendy's boyfriends called Kurt a "faggot" because Kurt didn't have a girlfriend. When Kurt finally did bring a girl home, and Wendy discovered them in bed together, Kurt was kicked out of the house. He was seventeen.

Kurt would later imply to the press that during this period he was living on the streets, sleeping in the damp spot under Aberdeen's Young Street Bridge after he got kicked out of his mom's house; he told the same story in the song "Something in the Way." Though he truly was homeless for a period, he did not live outside in Aberdeen's wet weather. "He never lived under that bridge," insists Krist Novoselic. "He hung out there, but you couldn't live on those muddy banks, with the tides coming up and down. That was his own revisionism."

Instead, Kurt slept on friends' porches, stayed in spare bedrooms, and when all other options failed, he slept in the heated hallways of apartment buildings. Most days he spent at the Aberdeen Timberland Library, where he educated himself by reading books like *The Outsiders* and *Catcher in the Rye*. He wrote a bit in his journal and played his guitar a little, but his artistic concerns were over-ridden by his survival needs. Simply finding a place to sleep and enough food to eat became daily challenges. Mostly, he relied on friends or the kindness of strangers, as he'd decided that no matter how desperate he became, he wanted nothing to do with his parents.

When he couldn't find a place to crash at night, he occasionally went back to Grays Harbor Community Hospital. This was the hospital where he was born, and he'd sneak in and sleep in the waiting room, pretending to be a bereaved relative. He displayed a degree of inventiveness in his street survival that was both inspiring and heartbreaking, and the emotional landscape he lived in would play an essential role in the songs he would later write. The neglect he felt, the abuse he suffered at the hands of the world, and the fear he lived with became, in a way, his unique story to tell. Though the song "Something in the Way" was an exaggeration of Kurt's actual circumstances, it did capture a larger intimate truth: He felt unwanted, and, to a degree, he was.

BACK IN THE SUMMER OF 1983, two years before he became homeless, Kurt's artistic life had gotten a jolt when he witnessed his first punk rock concert. The setting was the parking lot of the only grocery store in Montesano, and the band was the Melvins. Describing the event in his journal, Kurt saw this singular moment as the turning point that forever set him in the direction of punk rock. "They played faster than I ever imaged music could be played, and with more energy than my Iron Maiden records could provide," he wrote. "*This was what I was looking for.* Ah, punk rock. The other stoners were bored and kept shouting, 'Play some Def Leppard.' God, I hated those fucks more than ever. I came to the promised land of a grocery store parking lot and I found my special purpose."

The Melvins concert represented Kurt's "Eureka!" moment. It wasn't just the music that drew him in, however: The very idea of punk rock gave Kurt an identity that celebrated his outcast status. His troubled family life was punk; so were his drug use, his art, and his depression. To a rock critic, punk rock means a style of raw music that emphasizes emotion and dissonance over sentiment, but to Kurt, the label was one that could be used to define anything outside the mainstream. To Kurt, punk rock's most useful purpose was to give a name—and a justification—to his differentness.

Punk music, however, had to grow on Kurt, and his friends recall that he still listened to the same Def Leppard albums he criticized as being mainstream. In a sign that punk did not immediately grab him, his next concert after the Melvins was a Judas Priest show he witnessed at the Tacoma Dome Arena. Still, Kurt slowly began to explore what punk rock meant as an aesthetic choice. Roger "Buzz" Osborne, the leader of the Melvins, would loan Kurt punk albums, which were passed back and forth among Aberdeen's teens as if they were sacred objects. Those borrowed vinyl discs exposed Kurt to a larger musical world than Top 40 radio. With his limited funds, Kurt began to buy records of his own, and that collection became one of his first ways to express himself musically. It was also one of the first times that physical items—albums, in this case—became part of his unique identity.

The Melvins' practice space became a frequent hangout for Kurt, and he slowly changed his fashion attire to reflect his new allegiance. The polo shirts of the year before were out, replaced by homemade T-shirts that he had emblazoned with slogans. One read "Organized Confusion," which he was kicking around as a possible name for the band he wanted to form. He was morphing into a punk rocker, and his appearance dramatically shifted. Many of his old friends no longer recognized him as he began to wear a black trench coat and grow out his hair. As for shoes, he wore only Converse tennis shoes, a preference that he would maintain for the rest of his life.

Kurt later said that he had "tried out" for the Melvins (and had been rejected) and that he had served time as "a roadie" for the band. Both descriptions were exaggerations, but the claim that he failed their auditions furthered his punk status as an outcast even among outcasts. While Kurt did

RIGHT A thirteen-year-old Kurt visiting his aunt Mari. It was at her house that he would have his first recording session.

jam with the Melvins, there was never a formal audition. As for a job as a roadie, Kurt might have carried an amp a time or two, but the Melvins didn't travel by tour bus or with formal roadies; instead, they had a group of fans they called the "Cling-Ons," who accompanied the band with their infamous "Mel-Van," an ancient Dodge van they used to carry their gear.

Though Kurt was already practicing the guitar, aspiring to a Melvin-like sound, he was better known around Aberdeen for his art skills than his guitar prowess. Perhaps his greatest contribution around that time to the Melvins' legacy was as their in-house band artist. He often made posters and flyer designs for the band and talked about making T-shirts for them. But his largest involvement came when he painted part of the Mel-Van. He adorned it with an image of the band KISS, and lettered the Melvins' name in a style that imitated the KISS logo. Even though Melvins gigs were infrequent, the van was seen many places as the band members drove to work or practice. Kurt Cobain was virtually unknown as a musician at the time, but by painting the Mel-Van, he found his first small degree of infamy in the Grays Harbor punk rock community.

DURING JUNIOR HIGH AND HIGH SCHOOL, art was the only class Kurt consistently enjoyed. Many times he would skip all his morning classes, but then later return to school grounds for art period. He had a series of art teachers who mentored him, and the class was one of the few places in his life where he found recognition and self-respect.

In 1985, Kurt's art teacher, Bob Hunter, encouraged him to enter the Regional High School Art Show. His painting—a landscape—was selected as a finalist and entered into a statewide competition. Kurt's work lost at the state level, but he did come away with a certificate. From the way he talked about the award, however, his friends got the impression he'd won a million dollars; later in his life, Kurt amended the story to say he'd "won" the contest.

But it is not an exaggeration to say that art was the only subject in high school where Kurt excelled. "He had both the ability to draw, coupled with a great imagination," Bob Hunter recalled. At the time, Kurt's primary stylistic techniques were realism or caricature, but his subject choice was always a little odd. For one caricature assignment, he crafted a picture of Michael Jackson moonwalking, but holding his crotch in a sexualized way while doing so. Another assignment was to show an object evolving over time: Kurt took the assignment literally and drew a sperm cell turning into an embryo. An assignment on lettering found him re-creating the logo of the Fender guitar. A class segment on portraiture produced one of his most remarkable early paintings: He drew a takeoff of Grant Wood's *American Gothic* but substituted two punked-out senior citizens for Wood's farmers. The grandpa sported a Mohawk, a leather jacket, and earrings, while the grandma had a haircut right out of the eighties synth rock group A Flock of Seagulls.

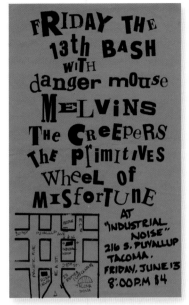

LEFT Long before Kurt had any renown as a musician, he was best known in Grays Harbor as the kid who painted the KISS drawings on the side of the Melvins' van, known to locals as the "Mel-Van."

ABOVE Two posters from shows by the Melvins, Kurt's greatest early influence. At the time, finding locations for punk rock concerts was difficult enough that bands often played in nontraditional venues like warehouses, which required maps on the advertisements.

When he wasn't completing a project for class, Kurt was doodling. Most of these crude drawings depicted typical boy stuff, like guitars, cars, trucks, and band logos, but he also drew pornography. "He once showed me this sketch that he'd drawn," said classmate Bill Burghardt, "and it was a totally realistic picture of a vagina." Oversized penises were also a favorite theme for Kurt. Many times, evil horned devils sported giant phalli, and Satan was a reoccurring character in Kurt's doodles. Aliens and extraterrestrial beings often appeared, and even a realistic picture of a human might contain an alien looking out from the background.

Though Kurt later claimed that by fifteen he had already decided he was going to be a rock star, in high school he was more likely to tell an inquirer that commercial art was his chosen field. He drew so many cartoons—often at the request of his friends—he began to imagine he could forge a career as a cartoonist. He talked about attending art school, and he later told journalists that he had been offered a scholarship, a boast that was completely without truth. Teachers like Bob Hunter suggested that if Kurt applied himself, art school might be a possibility, but the rest of his grades were so below par that college—even art college—was out of the question. Kurt had fallen so far behind academically that his friends teased him by converting "Cobain" into the nickname "Slow-Brain."

In his cartoons, Kurt began to explore the idea of storytelling, and what he learned to do on the page would later affect his songwriting. A series of characters regularly appeared in his cartoons, including "Jimmy, the Prairie Belt Sausage Boy," named for a canned meat product, and a transparent personification of Kurt himself; "Mr. Moustache," an obvious attempt to poke fun at his father; "Crybaby Jerkins," a protesting whiner; and the duo of "The Fatman and Bobby," based on two Aberdeen misfits who, in real life, would occasionally buy beer for Kurt and his friends. These themes would also be reflected in his later songwriting: Usually his characters were confronting figures of authority, and they inevitably ended up triumphing by either ridiculing the rule-makers or killing them.

Kurt's desire to create and embellish could not always contain itself to the page. He became famous around Aberdeen for the graffiti that he drew in alleys or on the sides of businesses. "God Is Gay" was one of his favorite slogans, and he applied this to many an Aberdeen alleyway. Once, to annoy a neighbor, Kurt spray-painted the word "boat" on the man's speedboat; this was typical of Kurt's sense of humor, which was juvenile and sophomoric. The word "ack" spray-painted on the side of a building was enough to give him and his friends laughs for months, in part because it was so stupid. Aberdeen's police department considered graffiti a serious offense, and Kurt was arrested for it on at least one occasion.

There were not many opportunities for a freelance artist in Aberdeen, but Kurt decided to create a business charging kids for decorating skateboards. He put up flyers around town

ABOVE AND OPPOSITE By high school, aliens had become one of Kurt's favorite art subjects. Whether he was drawing with marker or using paint, as with these two examples, long-limbed extraterrestrials were a common topic in his artwork. He also began to use collage in many of his works, as illustrated at right with his incorporation of a yellow rose cut out of a magazine.

FLAP Kurt may have been more proud of this art show certificate than he was of any other artistic award he received during his lifetime; although he didn't win the show, this recognition had a lasting effect on his artistic confidence.

FOLLOWING Kurt in his bedroom at his mother's home in Aberdeen in the late eighties. Once he received his beloved guitar, music became his obsession. Though several flyers for punk shows are on the walls, his UCLA T-shirt and the albums in his collection—including Creedence Clearwater Revival's *Cosmo's Factory* on the left—reflected more pedestrian tastes.

advertising this trade, and one potential customer phoned Kurt. The kid wanted to see if Kurt could create an exploding head on his skateboard. It was exactly the kind of motif Kurt specialized in, and he methodically came up with several designs, anxious to start what he imagined would be a lucrative career. But the customer never called back, nor did anyone else. The exploding head remained nothing more than an image in a notebook, left behind on a page among Kurt's many ideas for grandeur. ■

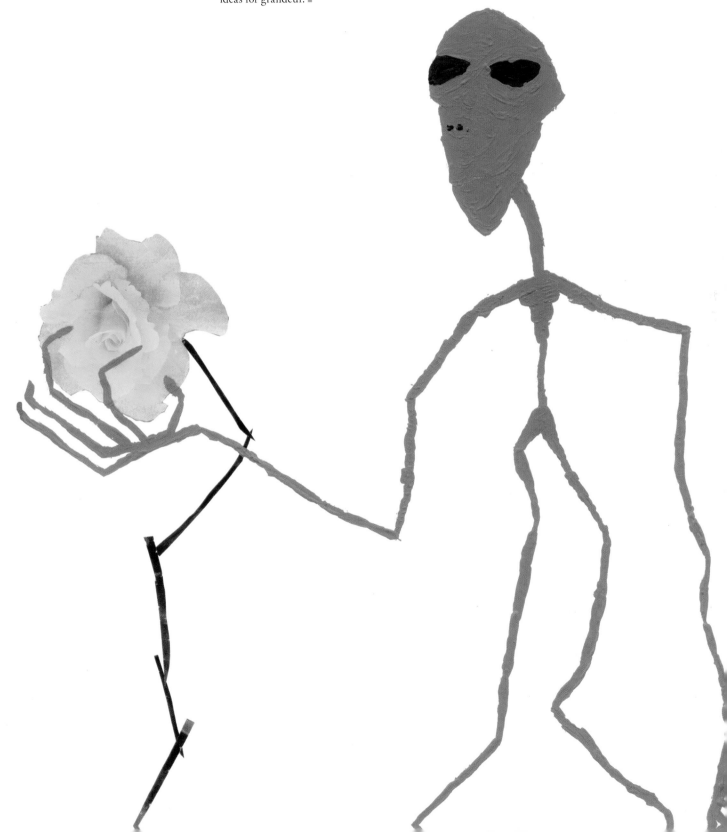

3

GUT BOMB

By the time Kurt began high school, he had added songwriting to his creative repertoire. His first attempts were more crude sound experiments than traditional narratives, but they represented a shift of his larger creative process toward a focus on musical expression.

The first extant recordings of Kurt date to when he was just two, when his aunt Mari recorded him screaming into the microphone "Hey, monkey." Other early family tapes capture him singing "Hey Jude," Arlo Guthrie's "Motorcycle Song," and the theme to the television show *The Monkees*.

Mari had recording equipment in her house, and when Kurt became a teenager, he regularly visited his aunt to use the gear. In December of 1982, when he was fifteen, he recorded his first proper "demo," putting the name "Organized Confusion" on the session. Kurt played all the instruments himself, using wooden spoons and a suitcase for percussion. Mari recalled that most of those songs were heavily distorted and Kurt's voice was muddled and distant.

In December 1985, Kurt structured a more formal session at Mari's, using drummer Dale Crover from the Melvins on bass and neighbor Greg Hokanson on drums. Kurt called this group "Fecal Matter," and it was his first nascent band. Kurt arrived with a spiral notebook stuffed full of songs. A handful of those songs survived long enough to become Nirvana tracks, but most were embryonic experiments done in a nihilistic style that owed much to the Melvins. Titles included "Suicide Samurai," about a depressed assassin; "Bambi Slaughter," a tale of a boy selling his parents' wedding rings; "Buffy's Pregnant," about the character from the *Family Affair* television show; "Downer," an angry rant about the sorry state of American culture; "Spank Thru," an ode to masturbation; and "Sound of Dentage," a bizarre noise experiment. Kurt had written lyrics to most of the tracks, but few were completed to his satisfaction during the session. He was more in love with the cleverness of the band name, Fecal Matter, than he was with the final recording. Nonetheless, he produced a cassette tape, which he proudly gave to friends in Aberdeen.

RIGHT An image from the very first photo session Nirvana ever conducted, for their debut Sub Pop single. Kurt wore a Harley Davidson T-shirt, despite the fact that he was far too concerned with safety to actually ride a motorcycle. Self-conscious of his acne, Kurt was pleased that many of Alice Wheeler's shots were done with infrared film, which distorted his appearance.

You will need to have the attached IDENTIFICATION CARD with you whenever you obtain food coupons or do your food shopping. Please sign the Identification Card and keep it in a safe place so that it will be available each time you go to get your coupons or buy food. If your spouse, a responsible member of your household or an authorized representative designated by you will be picking up your coupons or buying your groceries, PRINT his/her name on the reverse of this card in the space provided. BOTH OF YOU MUST THEN SIGN THE CARD.

WASHINGTON STATE
DEPARTMENT OF
SOCIAL & HEALTH
SERVICES

COMMUNITY SERVICES DIVISION
FOOD STAMP PROGRAM · IDENTIFICATION CARD

I S S U E D   T O

14 F 87629-0   NO
                   14

COBAIN,KURT D
707 W. MARKET #5
ABERDEEN, WA 98520

< (DETACH ALONG PERFORATIONS)

_____
          SIGNATURE
DSHS 12-04(X) (Rev. 4-82 -360-   **KEEP THIS CARD—DO NOT DESTROY**

The band Fecal Matter, insomuch as it was a band, only played a handful of rehearsals. "We played Hendrix and Monkee covers, and we even did an Elvis song," recalled Greg Hokanson. "Kurt had already written a bunch of original stuff. He'd been writing stuff in notebooks for years."

The Fecal Matter tape, however, did play an essential role in the genesis of Nirvana. One of the recipients of the tape was another Aberdeen misfit named Krist Novoselic. Novoselic was two years older than Kurt and was working at the local Burger King when Kurt stopped by to talk with him about music. When Krist heard the tape, one song impressed him. "It had 'Spank Thru' on it," Krist recalled. "I thought it was a really good song."

Kurt had spent much of the previous year shuttling between a handful of unofficial foster-home families, as he continued to struggle with both his external life—where to live—and his internal psychology. He had dropped out of high school and briefly attended an alternative school only to drop out of that. His level of desperation was great enough that he twice considered joining the navy, and he spent several weeks as a born-again Christian. Not long after he'd joined a church youth group, he was just as suddenly un-born.

After quitting school, Kurt worked several jobs, including stints as a dishwasher and as a janitor at his high school, but he'd been unable to keep any job for long and was surviving only with food stamps. He rented an apartment for a few months but was kicked out when he couldn't come up with the $85 a month in rent. When Novoselic and his girlfriend, Shelli Dilley, discovered that Kurt had been sleeping in an old refrigerator box on a buddy's porch, they offered to let Kurt stay behind their house in their camper van. It was a small kindness but one that Kurt never forgot.

Bassist Novoselic became not only Kurt's musical foil but also the first disciple to share Kurt's peculiar vision of the world. They talked often about the corruption of mainstream culture and how they might alter the course of things with their anarchistic musical ideas. The large antiestablishment themes that Kurt repeatedly talked about—challenging authority, corrupting the mainstream—were also obsessions of Novoselic's, so the two were ideologically well matched.

Their concept for taking over the mainstream culture, however, had not yet been perfected, and it says much that their very first group was organized as a desperate attempt to make some money from music. They had observed that Creedence Clearwater Revival was a perennially popular band on the radio, at that point two decades after their initial hit-making. Kurt and Krist decided that if they formed a Creedence cover band they could become wealthy. When this failed to advance their careers, they formed a series of other bands, though to even describe them formally by any name is a stretch, as they were more embryonic bands than real groups. One incarnation that actually progressed to a name and a few rehearsals was "The Stiff Woodies"—as was typical with Kurt, the name had sexual connotations. The band often practiced above Novoselic's mother's hair salon

TOP LEFT Kurt, pictured around the time he moved to Olympia, standing in view of the Washington State Lottery office, which he often shot at with a BB gun.

BOTTOM LEFT Kurt's food stamp card. For several years, while living in both Aberdeen and Olympia, Kurt was poor enough to qualify for public assistance.

In his notebooks, he wrote out lists of potential band names with candidates that included Poo Poo Box, Egg Flog, Whisker Biscuit, Spina Bifida, Puking Worms, and Pukearrhea. Kurt convinced neighbor Aaron Burckhard to sign on as drummer, and when a friend organized a house party in Raymond, Kurt's band had their first show. They didn't play under any name, but then the circumstances didn't require one since the beer at the party was more important than the entertainment. The gig was a near catastrophe: As Kurt sang, a drunk Krist Novoselic kept jumping out of the windows of the house. A fight ensued, and the night came to a premature close. While the band made no money from the show, it whetted Kurt's appetite for more.

SOON AFTER THE RAYMOND DEBUT, Kurt moved to Olympia to live with Tracy. He was twenty years old, and other than a childhood trip to Disneyland and an occasional visit to Seattle, he had never left Grays Harbor County. Olympia was a college town, as it was home to the Evergreen State College, and, in Kurt's mind, offered more opportunities. Though he attempted to find employment and briefly worked as a janitor in Olympia, he mostly lived off Tracy's kindness, which suited his slothful nature. When anyone challenged him to get a real job, his response was that the requirements of his band were so great he didn't have the free time.

By that point, the band had only played a handful of shows, mostly in Tacoma, to crowds no bigger than a dozen people. They had performed under a few different names—usually as Skid Row—until Kurt finally settled on Nirvana. A poster for one of the first shows performed under the moniker Nirvana even came with the footnote, "Also known as Skid Row, Ted Ed Fred, Pen Cap Chew, and Bliss." Kurt designed that poster, as he did most of their advertisements, and it featured a buxom Virgin Mary with bleeding hands. Images of Mary and Jesus often showed up in Kurt's art—he also frequently stole sculptures of Mary from graveyards. Once he had this contraband in his house, he'd doctor it by painting bloody tears on the face of the Virgin Mary. He stole crosses from cemeteries and put those on the walls as well.

As for the name Nirvana, Kurt was attracted to the Eastern mysticism it suggested, but mostly he picked it because it sounded sophisticated. Almost all of the other names he considered came from scatological references. Skid Row referenced "skid marks," fecal stains on underwear, rather than a desolate street. His first group had been called Fecal Matter. The fact that he managed to name the band Nirvana, and not Gut Bomb, as he had at one point insisted, was a minor miracle.

The human body—in particular its waste removal system—was an endless source of fascination for Kurt. Colons, enemas, anuses, stomachs, intestines, and feces were topics that he wrote about extensively in his journals and considered legitimate subjects for songs. Combined with sexuality—specifically birth, semen, and embryos—the anatomical world accounted for 90 percent of the themes he wrote about and the art he created.

Some of that interest was from medical necessity, as since childhood Kurt had suffered from various stomach ailments. He would often vomit bile. He believed that vegetables irritated his system and that cheese products were soothing—though those choices were the opposite of what most gastroenterologists would have suggested.

After moving to Olympia, he sought out a specialist for his troubles and was given a diagnosis of Irritable Bowel Syndrome (IBS). Little was known about IBS in 1988, and it often was the diagnosis given when other treatable ailments had been ruled out. Kurt's IBS, as typical of the disease, did not often follow a pattern or respond to one simple treatment. For Kurt, this meant he lived with the maddening prospect of inflammation that came seemingly at random. It was, he wrote in his journal, "Like Russian roulette, and I never know when it will come on. I can be at home in the most relaxed atmosphere, sipping natural spring water, no stress, no fuss, and then wham! Like a shotgun: stomach time is here again."

Kurt had also suffered from scoliosis since childhood. This condition, caused by a curvature of the spine, can be debilitating to many, but Kurt's case was not considered serious enough for a brace. It did, however, lead to irregular back pain and times when Kurt said his "bones ached." Kurt felt that wearing a heavy guitar exacerbated it, yet he played the guitar for hours every day, no doubt worsening the condition.

Kurt had always been thin, but his inability to gain weight increased along with his stomach problems. He felt insecure about his body and rarely let himself be seen naked. To bulk up his appearance, he frequently wore two or three shirts and two pairs of jeans. He undertook these fashion choices as a form of deception; later they would spark a fashion trend when he became famous.

Almost any person battling two chronic physical diseases would have struggled, but when mixed with depression, the frustration of his gut issues was almost too much for Kurt to bear. He saw his ailments not simply as impediments to be overcome but as curses. "You're cursed. . . . You've worked harder than anyone in the world," he wrote in one journal entry. He went on to lament dozens of things wrong in the world before concluding with what accounted for small comfort in Kurt's dark world: "I don't blame you for being bitter."

UNTIL 1988, THE BAND HAD EXISTED mostly as a phantom entity in Kurt's notebooks. Though Novoselic and Kurt frequently rehearsed, they struggled to find a consistent drummer. That didn't stop Kurt from writing hundreds of journal pages where he plotted out what his singular vision might be. Years before any journalist had any interest in interviewing him, he was writing out the

ABOVE Kurt's collection of strange junk included many board games and toys he purchased at thrift stores and garage sales, including this Shaun Cassidy doll, stored in its original box. He bought it as a gift for Tracy Marander, and it bears an inscription from him: "To Tracy, Love Kurdt."

RIGHT AND INSIDE FLAP Tracy Marander's photos of Kurt with one of their several cats and a rabbit in the backyard of their Olympia apartment.

answers he would give to what he considered the essential questions of rock. On the subject of punk rock, he wrote that he was for it, and that it "means freedom." He was also pro-"girls with weird eyes" and liked "nature and animals." If he had a fault, it was simply that he "liked to taunt small barking dogs in parked cars." As for these and other preferences, well, he simply had "strong opinions with nothing to back them up with besides my primal sincerity." The fake question-and-answer dialogues were amusing but also showed an intelligence beyond the sophomoric humor.

Kurt had written a couple dozen songs by now, but he obsessively wrote lists of the song titles in his notebooks, planning sequences for albums that would never be produced. In the middle of a list of potential cuts for an album, his girlfriend, Tracy, might write him a note—Kurt's journal was also used for to-do lists and grocery store reminders—like one that had a heart and read, "Please feed the rats." Yet, Kurt mostly filled his journals with the band's business, which existed almost entirely in his head.

In Nirvana's few gigs up to that point, the band had used three different drummers; they had the most luck borrowing Dale Crover from the Melvins. Kurt was still running ads looking for a permanent drummer, even as they played gigs with Crover. It says much about Nirvana's dim hopes at the time that Crover never seriously considered leaving the Melvins for Kurt's band, despite Crover's close friendship with Kurt. In the October 1987 issue of *The Rocket,* Kurt placed the following classified: "SERIOUS DRUMMER WANTED. Underground attitude, Black Flag, Melvins, Zeppelin, Scratch Acid, Ethel Merman. Versatile as heck. Kurdt 352-0992."

Not only was *The Rocket* ad significant because it showed the nascent band was still searching for a drummer—and a way to distinguish its sound—but it was also the first printed evidence of Kurt's playful, artful alter ego. He began to misspell his name by adding a "d" or an extra "t," or switching the "K" to a "C," or by doing the opposite and turning his last name into "Kobain." The "Kurdt Kobain" moniker wasn't exactly a stage name and was only occasionally used in correspondence to anyone he knew well; writing a note to Tracy, he would rarely use the ridiculous "Kurdt" spelling. Yet for a press bio, it was more likely than not that Kurt would misspell his name in some way. The misspellings themselves weren't consistent, and the motivation went unaddressed by Kurt. It may have been that he was attempting to find a stage name, or perhaps he thought a slightly different professional name would separate his artistic life from his real one. It also may simply have been one of Kurt's stupid jokes—this coming from a man who spray-painted the word "boat" in three-foot-tall letters on the side of his neighbor's speedboat.

Around this time, Kurt responded to an ad in *The Rocket* offering up recording studio time for $20 an hour. Producer Jack Endino, who answered the phone and produced the session, knew so little about Nirvana that his entry in the schedule read "Kurt Covain." In six hours, Kurt, Krist

ABOVE Kurt in the kitchen of his Olympia apartment. He said he enjoyed cooking, despite his lifelong stomach problems.

RIGHT One of Kurt's journal entries about his mother. Her attractiveness and his friends' flirty comments about her confused his own sense of sexuality and shame. Below the journal entry is a binder cover on which Kurt has outlined the songs from his first demo. Simply writing song lists was an activity that occupied much of Kurt's time during the era when the band had few gigs.

the Lady whom I feel A
maternal love for cannot look
me in the eyes
but I see hers and they
are Blue and they cock
& twitch & masturbate

very later I I have learned
to accept some friends
of ridicule my whole
existence was for your amusement

SHABA-DOO

IF YOU MUST
DOWNER
floyd the Barber
Paper Cuts
SPANK THRU
HAIRSPRAY Queen
Aeroszeppelin
~~Business your own mind~~ Beeswax
MEXICAN Seafood
PEN CAP CHEW
ANNOREXORCIST
ERECTUM

New weird

Novoselic, and Dale Crover recorded and mixed nine and a half songs, completing what has become known as the "Dale Demo." When a reel of tape ran out during the last song, "Pen Cap Chew," Kurt decided against spending $30 for another reel of tape to redo it. Kurt paid the $152.44 bill with money he'd saved from a brief janitorial stint, and the band left for a show they had that night in Tacoma. This simple session would become the first chapter in the legend of Nirvana in the studio; several songs from the inexpensive Dale Demo would eventually be officially released and consequently heard by millions of fans.

Kurt's lyric writing was becoming more focused, though the topics still reflected his typical obsessions: angst, sexuality, stomach pain, and television. "Floyd the Barber" was one of the most linear songs cut that day and recounted getting a shave from Floyd, the barber from *The Andy Griffith Show*. Floyd begins shaving the protagonist until the singer hears "a zip" and feels Floyd's "pee pee pressed against my lips." Later the singer dies, "smothered in Andy's butt." That this song was the *most* straightforward of the ten recorded that day says much about the vivid imagination of Kurt Cobain. Given the typical punk mixing of the guitar and bass above the lyrics, few listeners would have had any idea of what words Kurt was shouting. As with most of the songs on the Dale Demo, the subject of the song would have been almost impossible for a casual listener to determine without a lyric sheet.

Kurt's stomach was referenced in "Mexican Seafood," a song that detailed a variety of ailments from "a yeast infection" to gonorrhea ("only hurts when I pee"), and ends with "Toe jam and booger / stomach acid worms / that dance in sugared sludge." As for the inspiration behind Kurt's other odd lyrics, even he was at a loss to explain what he wrote about. In one of Nirvana's earliest interviews, a journalist asked Kurt what his lyrics were about. It was one of the few questions he hadn't already rehearsed an answer for in his phantom notebook interviews. "I don't consider lyrics a big deal at all, as long as it has a good melody line," he replied. "A hook and live energy are far more important."

However strange the lyrics were, Kurt was crafting catchy melodies, and it was this element that intrigued Sub Pop's Jonathan Poneman. When producer Jack Endino passed along the demo tape to Poneman, the label head offered the band a record deal. Officially, it was little more than a handshake agreement in which Poneman promised Sub Pop would pay the minimal recording costs to cut a single. The band was given no advance but would get one hundred copies of the single. To Kurt, the record deal, and most specifically the fact that he could tell people he had signed to a label, ranked with his 1985 art show "win" as one of the most glorious occurrences of his life. ∎

LEFT Kurt was fascinated with meat; he cut out numerous color pictures from magazines, which he used to make collages. Part of this layout was attached to the refrigerator in his Olympia apartment.

By early 1988, Chad Channing joined Nirvana as drummer, and things began to solidify for the band. With the Sub Pop deal and a handful of shows in Seattle, they seemed to have momentum, or so Kurt argued. In his journals, he wrote several bios for what he called "our little band," revising them as soon as he had any new nugget of good news. Still, the breaks came slower than he would have liked, and it wasn't until November of 1988 when Sub Pop finally released the "Love Buzz" single. Even that glorious occasion was fraught with complications for Kurt, as the reviews were not the unqualified raves Kurt had hoped for. The single was only issued initially as part of a subscription club, and several reviewers despairingly noted that it was a cover of a Shocking Blue song, an odd choice for debut.

During most of 1988, Kurt waited: for Sub Pop to act, for the band to get more shows, for the new lineup to jell, or for Tracy to come home from work. He spent most of his time by himself in their Olympia apartment watching television, making mixed tapes, or writing songs. When Tracy complained that he'd written songs about everything but her, he took his first stab at crafting a love song. While listening to *Meet the Beatles*, he sat in his bathtub and wrote out an argument he'd had with Tracy the week before, turning the dialogue into a song.

Around the same time, Kurt wrote "Negative Creep," which was more typical of the period. Most Nirvana songs were structured around guitar chords, rather than driven by lyrics, and "Negative Creep" had only ten lines, though each was repeated three times. Other than the chorus of "Daddy's little girl ain't a girl no more," repeated twenty-seven times, few of the lyrics were decipherable. Kurt went into the recording studio without having completed the song, and once the tape was rolling, he ended several couplets with a screaming whine that was fast becoming his vocal trademark and the signature of the band's sound. The songs were undeniably catchy, but their meanings were a mystery even to Kurt's bandmates.

Though Kurt was writing at a faster pace than ever before, Sub Pop's financial problems held up the recording of a real album. He had expected his band to have two albums out already, and all

RIGHT This Alice Wheeler photograph of Kurt was originally considered for the cover of *Bleach*, but Kurt rejected it. There were at least three photo sessions for the album cover, but in the end the band chose a live shot printed in the negative so that none of the members were recognizable.

Sub Pop had done was issue the single. Frustrated, Kurt began to send out demo tapes to other labels. With one package, Kurt included a handwritten bio that noted Nirvana was "willing to *compromise* on material (some of this shit is pretty old). Tour any time forever. Hopefully the music will speak for itself. Please reply." He had previously railed against compromise, but the long delay had made him increasingly desperate.

In December 1988, Sub Pop finally managed to budget for recording costs, and the band cut their first album with producer Jack Endino. Kurt debated a number of titles including *Mandatory Breeding Laws*, *All Humans Are Stupid*, and *Ashamed to Be a Human*. The one he liked best was *Too Many Humans*, which reflected his pessimistic view of overpopulation. Sub Pop axed that idea, so Kurt decided to name it *Bleach*. On tour for the single, Kurt had seen an AIDS prevention poster with the line, "Bleach Your Works." Kurt had not experimented with hard drugs at this time, and he found the line humorous. For a design, the group decided to use a band photo Tracy had taken, but to print it in negative. The cover was also meant to be a play on "Negative Creep," but few would have gotten that joke.

BLEACH WAS RELEASED ON JUNE 15, 1989, whereupon the band undertook their first tour of the United States. Over the next three years, a season did not go by without Nirvana hitting the road. Their lives became structured around tours and shows, and it was the income from touring that kept them alive. College radio had picked up a few of the songs from *Bleach*, and though their first few tours lost money, they soon began to sell enough T-shirts to make a small profit.

ABOVE Drummer Chad Channing (left) and Kurt (right) wear Halloween masks on an early tour date. Chad was already the fourth drummer the band had used, but with the exception of Dave Grohl, Chad had the longest tenure. Many people mistook him and Kurt for brothers because of their similar appearance.

RIGHT Two flyers from Nirvana's early Seattle shows.

RIGHT BACKGROUND A contact sheet by photographer Charles Peterson from Nirvana's legendary show at the University of Washington's HUB Ballroom on February 25, 1989. The show was billed as "Four More Bands for Four More Bucks," meaning that attendees paid a dollar to see Nirvana.

BUNDLE OF HISS
NIRVANA
ЗА ЖИЗНЬ!
ЦѢНА 5 коп.

JUNE FIFTEEN
VOGUE
FIRST & VIRGINA

VOGUE

MARCH - APRIL CALENDAR

.... CRISIS PARTY / DERELICTS
.... ROGER MILLER / BUNDLE OF HISS
.... GOOD FRIDAY FOOLS PARTY
................PASSOVER OR PASSOUT
................PSYCHEDELIC EASTER
........FASTBACKS / SPLINTER PARTY
.... CATBUTT / SCHROEDINGERS CAT
.... THE RAD, THE BAD, THE 70'S
.... HOLY SISTERS OF THE GAGADADA
.... THE FIRST THOUGHT
.... DAS DAMEN / BLOOD CIRCUS
.......DHARMA BUMS / HERD OF TURTLES
............................SUBPOP w/ NIRVANA
.... CRYPT KICKER 5 / ACTION BUDDIE
.... NOMEANSNO record release

SHELTER VIDEO WELCOMES FROM
YORK SST RECORDING ARTISTS

DAS DAMEN
SPECIAL GUESTS BLOOD CIRCUS
AT THE DOOR. TUESDAY APRIL 19

N 9 TIL 2 AM OPEN AT 8 NOW ON FRI - SAT
SDAY LADIES FREE DAYLIGHT SAVINGS TIL 3

REPRODUCTION

TOP LEFT The band slept on couches and survived on pennies during their first tour of the U.S. in 1989. Here, Kurt wears an overcoat, though they were traveling in July. No matter how balmy the weather, he wore several layers of clothes.

CENTER LEFT Kurt claimed he drank Strawberry Quik because it coated his stomach, which acted up when he was on the road.

BOTTOM LEFT Nirvana live at Green Street Station in Massachusetts, July 1989.

ENCLOSURE The band had so little money for promotion that Kurt decided to make homemade stickers. He methodically wrote out the band's name on hundreds of these Avery computer labels. A handful of his original stickers can still be found on walls and alleyways in Olympia.

ABOVE In an age before eBay, Kurt collected hundreds of games and lunch boxes. His *Adam-12* lunch box was one of his favorites.

To Kurt, making money on his music was sweet justice. He was still primarily living off Tracy, but now he had a few extra dollars for his own whims. When he wasn't touring, he stayed at home and watched television or worked on a variety of art projects. He'd begun to haunt Olympia's many thrift stores, and he started to buy anything weird and cheap that struck his fancy. He had a particular fascination with board games, which he could usually buy for less than a dollar. He wasn't interested in Sorry! or Scrabble, but if the game was a knockoff of a bad TV show, he'd buy it. The castoffs of sixties culture became his fixation: He bought an Archie Bunker board game, an *Adam-12* game, and an *A-Team* game. He became a curator of the absurd debris of American pop culture. He bought a cheap tapestry of Elvis and then doctored it by putting makeup in the style of Alice Cooper on Elvis's face; he then rechristened it "Elvis Cooper." The band hung the Elvis Cooper tapestry behind them during some shows, and it became a hit with their then tiny audiences. Everything Kurt created or bought was abnormal in a way or was soon made that way through his doctoring.

Kurt's interest in painting re-emerged that summer, and since he couldn't afford real canvas, he often used the backs of these old board games. He found that the stiff cardboard held acrylic paint well. He also occasionally bought cheap, framed paintings at the thrift store and then repainted the canvases or altered them in some way. Sometimes he'd simply take the store-bought painting and paint words over it.

He gave Tracy several of the original paintings he created that year. One was of a skeletal, alienlike being looking forlorn—Kurt told Tracy it was a self-portrait. Another was of convicted murderer Charles Manson. "He didn't paint happy-looking flowery stuff," Tracy observed.

One of his neighbors who admired his paintings offered to pay Kurt to re-create a dream she'd had. "How much do you charge?" the neighbor asked him. He had no idea, but he told her for ten dollars he could buy a canvas. She gave him the money and then described the dream, which was of a woman eating a dead animal. It took him a few days, but he captured her vision. It helped that most of Kurt's paintings were already ethereal and dreamlike, and that flesh-eating creatures were part of his oeuvre. The same neighbor once discovered him painting in the garage and noticed that the work glistened. She asked him what created the varnish effect. He matter-of-factly told her he'd masturbated and applied his semen as a final coat. "My seed is on this painting," he announced as drily as if he were describing a shade of color.

Sexuality remained a theme at the center of his art. He would search thrift stores for old medical texts, and then cut out anatomy pictures to create a collage. He decorated his refrigerator with pictures of diseased vaginas interspersed with photos of meat clipped from newspaper ads. If a headline appeared in the newspaper that had a double entendre (such as "Trojans beat Beavers"), he would clip it out and add it to the ever-evolving work. Collage was his favorite art form, and newspaper and magazine clippings were applied to anything flat he could find—a canvas, the refrigerator, or the wall.

Kurt also experimented with animated collage in the form of video editing: When Tracy bought a VCR, it became Kurt's favorite household appliance. He liked to tape clips from MTV, but mostly he filled countless inexpensive VHS tapes with late-night commercials and scenes from sixties reruns. He imagined that one day these video collages would be valuable. He recorded them all on economy mode, however, so even when he tried to play them back, they were distorted.

Though the VCR had been a bonding addition to their household, by late 1989, the relationship between Kurt and Tracy began to show strains. He was often gone touring, and while she truly was the biggest supporter Nirvana had—both financially and moralewise—living with Kurt wasn't easy for her. One of the other things they had in common was their love of animals, and their pets included turtles, rats, cats, and a rabbit. Kurt had nicknamed the apartment the "Animal Farm," and one visitor noted that it smelled "like a vivisection lab." Their menagerie required much care, and Kurt frequently was lax in cleaning their many pet cages; this and his other housekeeping lapses became relationship issues.

Tracy was a relatively straightforward woman and liked girlie things. Kurt's interest in femininity, however, was more confined to the porcelain dolls he collected or the stolen statues of the Virgin Mary he looted from cemeteries. For her birthday that year, he gave her an Iron Butterfly album. It wasn't just any album, though; he'd painted an image of Batman on it and tied to it a naked Barbie doll with a noose around its neck. To Kurt, this was romance.

Another issue between them was simply how much stuff Kurt had acquired on his thrift store jags. "He had this clutter thing," remembered Krist Novoselic. "His whole house was cluttered, and there were things everywhere." Tracy urged him to clean up, and repeatedly left him notes suggesting he do so. He ignored them, for the most part, and instead brought home more stuff. They had moved to a larger apartment in the same converted house, but Kurt quickly had packed the larger space with his ever-growing treasury.

ABOVE Photographer JJ Gonson's shot of Kurt inside Nirvana's van on their first East Coast tour captures him in his element. The photographer recalls that Kurt said he kept the crucifix in the van so that he could stick it out the window and shock pedestrians.

RIGHT Kurt took these two photographs of his crucifix with JJ Gonson in Nirvana's van and in front of McDonald's. The McDonald's image sums up the absurdity of American culture in a way that says much about Kurt's artistic vision.

ABOVE Though Kurt had a huge collection of toys, his favorite was a tiny monkey he had named Chim-Chim, after a character on the cartoon *Speed Racer*, who was obsessed with finding candy. Kurt had a number of Chim-Chim stickers, and he used the image as his unofficial mark.

ABOVE RIGHT In this photo, Chim-Chim sits in front of "Elvis Cooper," an Elvis poster Kurt had doctored to look like Alice Cooper.

RIGHT Kurt was an obsessive collector of toy monkeys, particularly ones of a musical nature. Over the course of his life he acquired dozens of them in every style, from inexpensive stamped metal toys to finely honed plush dolls. He kept many of these long enough that years later, when he became a father, he would often entertain his daughter with these toys.

NIRVANA'S FIRST TOUR OF EUROPE COMMENCED around the same time, compounding the stress at home in late 1989, but also giving Kurt a distraction. Nirvana found, much to the band members' surprise, that they had a following in Europe. The British music tabloids were always looking for a new star to tout, and Sub Pop's Mudhoney was the 1989 model of the year. While most of the early press on the Seattle grunge scene contained only anecdotal coverage of Nirvana, and many times it was unflattering reporting, calling them "hicks," there was enough ink on Sub Pop that fans came to see Nirvana out of curiosity. They were improving as a live unit, and Kurt's new songs were better at getting the crowd dancing or at least tapping its feet.

Even as Nirvana's popularity was slowly growing, Kurt continued to pursue other musical ventures, not yet completely willing to hitch his entire wagon to the idea of one band. When they came back from Europe, Kurt went into the studio to contribute material to a Mark Lanegan album, one of several times when Kurt joined a studio session with musicians outside of Nirvana. He'd also recorded some experimental music with the Go Team in Olympia, and right before the European tour, he'd even formed a minor offshoot group with a couple of the Screaming Trees. He called that band The Jury, and it included Kurt, Krist, Mark Lanegan, and Mark Pickerel from the Screaming Trees. Kurt conceived of this group as an opportunity for him to explore blues and folk music that might not fit into Nirvana's repertoire. At an August 1989 recording session, The Jury cut four Leadbelly songs, including "Where Did You Sleep Last Night" and "Grey Goose." Kurt also recorded a chilling solo version of "They Hung Him on a Cross." They had talked about continuing the band, but those 1989 recordings were the last of The Jury.

LEFT Kurt wearing an Iggy Pop and the Stooges T-shirt. He happened to wear this very shirt at a New York show that Iggy Pop himself attended, much to Kurt's eternal embarrassment.

TOP RIGHT Nirvana pictured moments before the Iggy Pop incident. Note the remarkable contrast in height between Krist Novoselic and the other two.

BOTTOM RIGHT One of Sub Pop's early promotional photos of Nirvana, taken by photographer Charles Peterson.

Still, Kurt's widening interest in blues and folk music proved that the "butt rock"—the AC/DC and Black Sabbath—he'd grown up on was now being supplemented by the albums he'd found in Olympia thrift shops or those borrowed from friends. His interest in Leadbelly reflected a notable move away from the punk stylings of the Melvins—where lyrics were an afterthought at best—toward traditional folk-song craft with a dominant narrative voice. What a song was *about* suddenly mattered to Kurt in a way it had not before, and his own writing mirrored this shift.

When he had been in Aberdeen, Kurt had found music mostly by happenstance—he'd hear it on the radio or hear another band covering a Zeppelin song. But in Olympia, Kurt began to explore a wider spectrum of music. He also sought out the advice of others, and there were many in the Olympia music community who were quick to suggest other albums he needed to explore. He lived next to Slim Moon and Dylan Carlson, and both were astute rock aestheticians who greatly influenced what Kurt discovered, as did Calvin Johnson who ran K Records. And as Kurt's record collection grew, it included albums by popular acts like the Beatles, Cheap Trick, The Knack, Devo, and Leonard Cohen, but also less obvious choices like the Vaselines and the Pixies. As Kurt's record collection expanded, so did his own musical style.

In the fall of 1989, Kurt took a handful of the new songs into the studio to record with producer Steve Fisk. The five tracks they cut over three days represented a remarkable leap in Kurt's songwriting prowess. "Polly," in particular, was the most sophisticated song Kurt had yet attempted. It was another twisted love song, but this time was written from the voice of a sexual deviant who kidnaps a young girl and tortures her. The criminal feels empathy for his victim but also displays a sociopathic detachment: "I think she wants some water to put out the blowtorch." Kurt wrote the song after reading a clipping in the newspaper of a similar real-life incident; the song represented one of the first times he'd reached outside his own imagination for source material.

Another of the five songs recorded that fall, "Been a Son," reflected Kurt's own family history. The song ostensibly tells the story of how Kurt believed his father would have preferred a more masculine son. The central character is female, so it is not clear whether Kurt wrote the song about his sister, Kim, or whether the lyrics, "she should have died when she was born," were more a statement of his own self-hate. But regardless of the inspiration, there was no mistaking the venomous anger. The song was a clear indication that Kurt had begun to use lyric writing as a form of therapy and release. Anger—at his parents, his health problems, and his own inner shame—became one of his most powerful motivators and part of his inspiration. Over the next year, Cobain's music would become more focused and, not surprisingly, would show a new level of fury. ■

NIRVANA

For someone who watched as much television as Kurt Cobain did, it was inevitable that one day he'd want to make his own music video. He'd created a number of Super 8 films, and also made numerous video collages with his VCR, but his first attempt at a music video didn't come until March 1990. With the help of a few college students, Nirvana sneaked on to the Evergreen State College campus for an afternoon-long video session. That they would imagine a zero-budget video would be shown on cable television displays their glorious naïveté. The results, while too amateurish to make MTV's cut, did prove wildly imaginative.

The band played for forty-five minutes in front of two cameras, while VHS footage Kurt had compiled played behind them on a chroma-key curtain. "He had taken Super 8 films of dolls, figures, broken toys, burning dolls, and stop-motion animated stuff that he had done himself," recalled Jon Snyder, who directed the session. Included on the tape were snippets of *Star Search* with Donny and Marie Osmond tap-dancing, *Fantasy Island*, Lee Press-On Nails commercials, and several hours of *The Power Team*, a show about Christian bodybuilders. Prior to the video session, Kurt had spent several nights editing down a stack of VHS tapes to find the perfect clips for a handful of songs. Both "School" and "Lithium" were recorded with Kurt's weird VCR clips in the background. For "Big Cheese," Kurt used silent footage from an obscure film on witchcraft, which he had purchased mail-order.

The final song, "Floyd the Barber," produced the strangest results of the day. This time, Kurt used footage of his doll creations for the background images. They were chilling, particularly a still of a porcelain doll turned on its head. As if that weren't weird enough, graphics were added during editing that made all three band members appear with multiple shadows. In addition to this, Novoselic had dressed in black pants, which the film editors realized made his legs disappear. To counter this, Krist put white duct tape on his pants in a crosswalk pattern, which like everything else was multiplied by the added effect. The final result was hypnotic, but completely minimized

RIGHT As Nirvana's success slowly built, Sub Pop hired noted photographer Michael Lavine to shoot the band in New York in April 1990. This shot captures Kurt just on the cusp of fame. Slightly over a year later, Lavine would also photograph the interior imagery for the *Nevermind* album.

ABOVE TOP Kurt and Chad on tour. On early trips Kurt didn't smoke or drink, and he was very careful about what he ate, so as not to upset his stomach.

ABOVE BOTTOM Kurt, Kim, and aunt Mari.

RIGHT This cartoon was folded into the pages of Kurt's journals, but unlike most of his writings from the era, it was written on a loose-leaf sheet rather than in a spiral notebook. The cartoon is titled "More Sarcasm" and plays off two themes Kurt was obsessed with: stereotypes within music culture and intestinal problems.

any musical statement the clip might have achieved. If Kurt had dreamed that a video was his immediate ticket to stardom, the results of the Evergreen shoot must have dashed his hopes.

The video, and several other band projects that year, marked a major transition in Kurt's artistic progress: The band was now big enough, and their projects complicated enough, that Kurt could no longer control their artistic output himself. Up until that point, he had been the one designing posters and logos, but now he and his bandmates required label executives, video directors, promotion staff, and producers. This changeover was difficult for Kurt to cope with, as he always wanted to do everything himself. Though he continued to draw in his notebooks, and write songs, the final artistic product of Nirvana was now reliant on external forces he was unable to control.

Not long after the video shoot, the band traveled to Madison, Wisconsin, to record their next album. Sub Pop had arranged for Butch Vig of Smart Studios to produce the record. Vig was a musician himself, not a heavy-handed producer, and he worked well with the band. They had only one week for the session but cut five new compositions, one cover (of the Velvet Underground's "Here She Comes Now"), and two songs they'd recorded before. The new tracks found Kurt continuing to use his own life as source material. "In Bloom" is a portrait of Dylan Carlson, Kurt's best friend. The lyrics, "He's the one / who likes all our pretty songs / and he likes to sing along / and he likes to shoot his gun," were a ribbing of Carlson, but done with affection. The song was the first example of a technique that Nirvana would perfect over the next year: the contrasting of soft and loud passages, usually achieved by playing a verse at a lesser volume and then cranking up the intensity and rhythm of the chorus.

The loud/soft technique was also used on "Lithium," which, of all the songs cut at Smart, was the one Vig thought held the most potential. The lyrics mock a religious conversion by an unstable personality. As he had on "Polly," Kurt chose to narrate the song in the first person: "I'm so happy 'cause today I found my friends." The manner in which he skewered the myopia of religious fundamentalism, while singing in a sympathetic tone that hid the sarcasm, showed Kurt's growing skills. By wedding the derisive lyrics with a melody that owed much to Cheap Trick, Kurt produced a nasty song that sounded sweet, a technique he would continue to perfect.

Two weeks after the Smart sessions, Kurt did a radio interview with a college station in Amherst, Massachusetts, where he addressed his songwriting's new direction. "The songs will be more pop-y sounding," he explained. When asked if he'd pursued that direction to get on the radio, Kurt replied, "Not at all. That has nothing to do with it. I like pop music."

Kurt began the interview by recounting a dream he'd had that he was under a "voodoo curse." He would fall asleep and not be able to move when he awoke. "I feel like I'm on the verge of dying because my lungs are collapsing." Beginning an interview by first mentioning that he

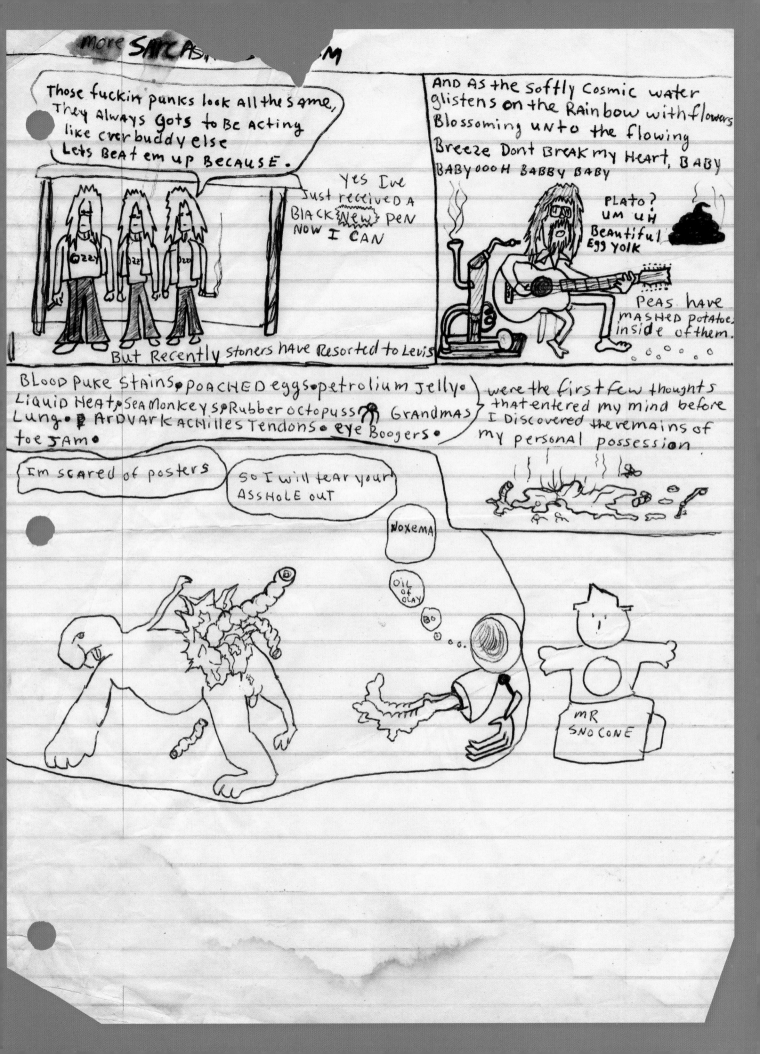

was "going insane" certainly helped make Kurt an interesting subject, but it also gave the band the kind of nihilistic edge that kept them on the pages of punk fanzines. Kurt was a fast study, so when he noticed that his outrageousness got as much attention as the practical matters of the band, he amplified that persona.

WHEN KURT RETURNED TO OLYMPIA, he spent hours drawing up track listings for the new album, which he wanted to title *Sheep*. He even coined an advertising slogan: "Nirvana. Flowers. Perfume. Candy. Puppies. Love. Generational Solidarity. And Killing Your Parents. *Sheep*." Two other titles he considered were *Sue Me* and *Happy*. In a sign that Kurt was still unsure of the direction of the band, one of his fake advertisements for *Sheep* was confessional: "Nirvana can't decide whether they want to be punk or R.E.M. Indecision can often at times kill a band and Nirvana are suicidal."

Kurt came home from the tour nearly suicidal himself. While irony and sarcasm marked almost everything Kurt created, the acme of his sarcastic wit may have been that he considered calling his album *Happy*. He was unhappy with virtually every aspect of his life. He went through this phase periodically; it stemmed, in all likelihood, from his depression. On the day the tour ended, he fired drummer Chad Channing from the band and broke up with Tracy. He soon regretted both decisions and was quickly more miserable than before, particularly after Tracy took the television with her.

With his benefactor gone, Kurt had to pay the rent himself. Without a drummer, the band couldn't play shows, which cut off Kurt's primary source of income. *Bleach* was earning royalties, but with Sub Pop slow to cut those checks, Kurt and Krist resorted to driving up to Seattle to demand quicker payment. The Smart sessions hadn't yielded enough songs to put out an album, and Sub Pop couldn't afford the pressing costs in any case.

Kurt once again had to look for a day job. Finding a position that would give him flexibility for the band wasn't easy. He reprised the idea of starting his own janitorial business, and he put up flyers for "Pine Tree Janitorial," thinking the company would soon dominate the commercial building maintenance market in Olympia. The flyers showed miniature bug-eyed caricatures of Kurt and Krist with mops in their hands. Kurt's marketing idea behind Pine Tree was that existing janitorial services were too busy to take on new customers. Since his business had no clients, he was better equipped, he argued. "Other services usually have too many buildings," he wrote in what amounted to his business plan. He went so far as to guarantee that Pine Tree's bid would be $50 lower than any other offer, but even that carrot failed to earn him any business.

Frustrated, he went back to placing advertisements for drummers and sending pleading letters to record companies. Sub Pop's glacial pace continued to infuriate Kurt, so he initiated contact with other labels. While there were no immediate takers, some tiny expressions of interest gave him hope,

LEFT September 23, 1990. By fall of 1990, Nirvana was big enough in the U.K. that journalists would fly over just for a few moments with the band. In this photo session, shot at Novoselic's Tacoma house, Kurt is wearing medical scrubs, one of his few pieces of clothing in addition to T-shirts and flannels.

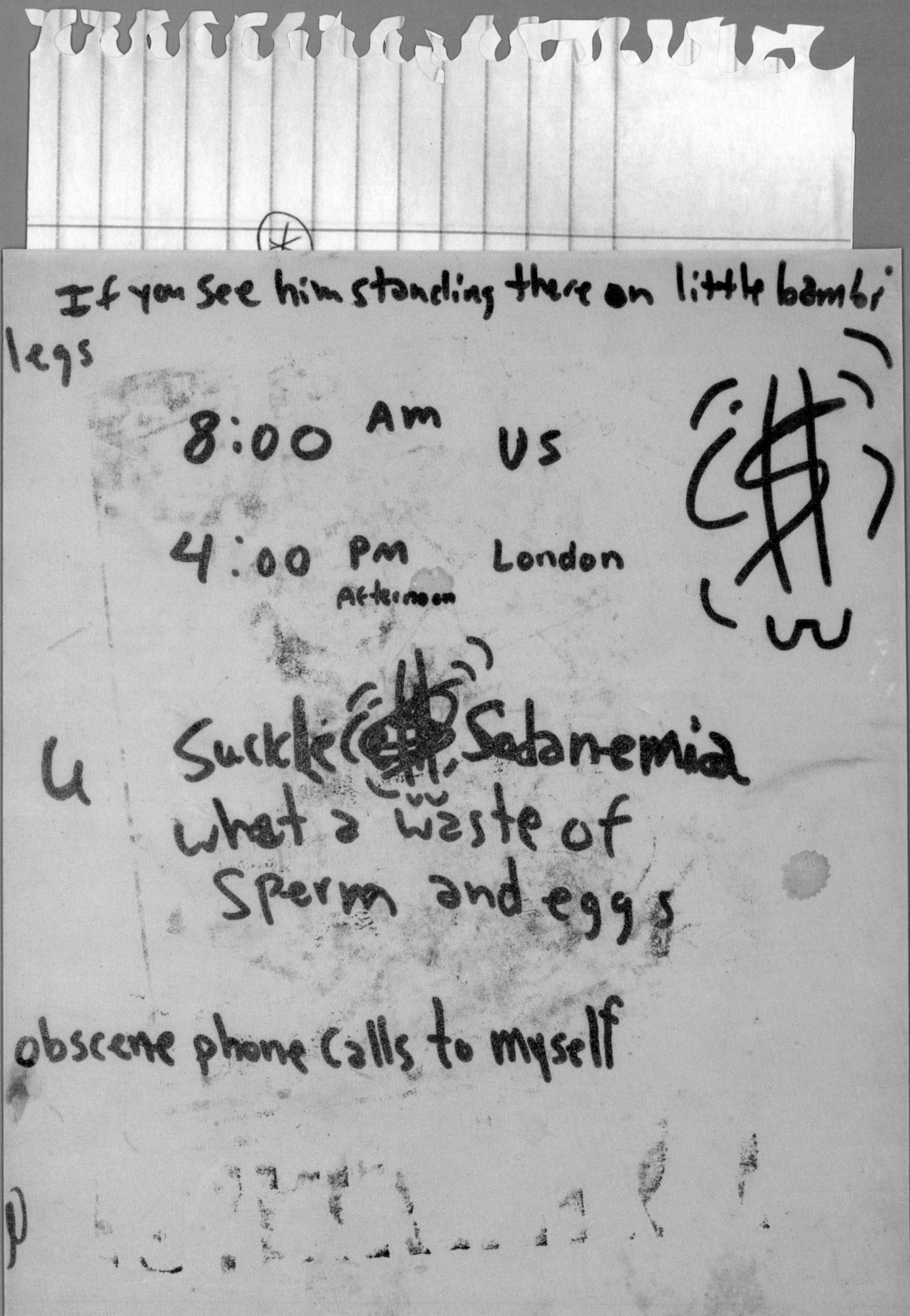

If you see him standing there on little bambi
legs

8:00 AM   US

4:00 PM   London
   Afternoon

4 Suckle Satanemia
   what a waste of
   sperm and eggs

obscene phone calls to myself

ENCLOSURE Kurt's handwritten draft of "Smells Like Teen Spirit." He wrote many versions, but even he didn't regard it as one of his strongest songs until after its release.

even if the drummer-less band barely existed that year. It would be three months before Nirvana would play live again, one of the longest dormant periods since they'd started.

That summer, Kurt began a short-lived relationship with Tobi Vail of the band Bikini Kill. He fell hard for her, and she became a quick muse for his songwriting, inspiring the line "Love you so much it makes me sick" in "Aneurysm." It was while he was dating Tobi that the infamous "Teen Spirit" graffiti came forth: To taunt Kurt about his crush, a friend wrote on his bedroom wall, "Kurt smells like Teen Spirit." It was meant in a teasing way; Teen Spirit was the name of a deodorant marketed to teenage girls, but Kurt didn't get the reference when he saw the line on his wall. "I had no idea what I was writing about," Kurt later said. He jotted down the slogan in his notebook and used it as the chorus of one of the many songs he crafted that summer. The graffiti didn't necessarily stand out in the apartment, as every wall had some kind of marking on it.

Kurt's relationship with Tobi was his first musical union with a female; they helped each other write melodies, worked on her fanzine, and talked about forming a band. They never actually formed a band, but they did fantasize about two titles for the group: "The Bathtub Is Real" and "Israeli Donkey." It was an odd relationship, with both of them later having different interpretations of what happened and what didn't. In the Olympia punk rock community, dating was looked down upon as traditional, so to her it was more "just hanging out," while to him it was a full-on courtship. When they split several months later, she recalled it as Kurt breaking it off with her, while his interpretation was the opposite; he told his friends he was brokenhearted.

That fall, Kurt had started to occasionally use hard drugs, specifically heroin. It was just experimentation at that point, and Kurt certainly didn't have enough money to use often, but it would have been a deal-breaker for Tobi, or for Tracy for that matter. Whether it was the desire to escape intimacy or the lack of intimacy that drove him to isolation, his drug usage pushed him further away from friends. He didn't attempt to hide his dabbling and went so far as to phone Novoselic and tell him he was using heroin.

His depression did spur on his creative drive, at least. Driven by lovesickness, stomach pain, and childhood hauntings, Kurt wrote a remarkable series of songs that summer. "Drain You" is one example, and it contains some of the most venomous lyrics he ever wrote. It was originally titled "Formula," then it became "The Retards," and finally "Drain You." While it started off with what might be a romantic, if codependent, sentiment—"I don't care what you think, unless it is about me"—the chorus was straight off Kurt's refrigerator collage of vaginas mixed with butcher shop ads: "Chew your meat for you / Pass it back and forth in a passionate kiss." If a line like "travel through a tube and end up in your infection" was meant as a valentine, it failed to woo its intended recipient.

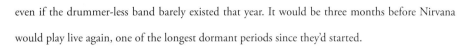

LEFT Some of the dozens of notebooks and journals that Kurt Cobain kept during his lifetime. Despite being homeless for several months and touring for many years, he managed to keep his treasure trove of writing together. This selection only represents a fraction of the number of notebooks Kurt was known to have kept; some were stolen, and many were damaged beyond repair when his apartment flooded in 1992. The fax on the left, printed on fading Sub Pop stationery, reads "Top Ten Reasons Kurt Cobain Is Gay." Number three is "He dyes his hair 'girlie' colors.'"

LEFT Kurt in his Olympia apartment, circa 1990. On the wall is the box for "The Visible Man" figure, and standing atop the lamp is one of the many models he collected. The end album on his record collection is one by the Butthole Surfers. Behind Kurt's left shoulder are miniature Beatles dolls he glued to the top of an amplifier. On the wall to the right is a Mikhail Gorbachev poster. All of the visual materials in Kurt's life affected and shaped his music and lyrics.

ENCLOSURE A Polaroid of Kurt wearing an International Pop Underground Festival T-shirt from Olympia and holding his kitten, Spina Bifida. Nirvana did not play at their hometown festival, marking the end of Kurt's relationship with the local scene.

In less than a month, he authored a dozen songs, several of which would become his best-known works. "Smells Like Teen Spirit" alone went through ten lyric drafts, but the basic themes—questioning authority, anger, blame—were repeated throughout. He had originally wanted to call the song "Anthem," but Tobi had written a song by that name, so he went with "Teen Spirit." "Neurotically lethargic," Kurt wrote on the side of one draft. "We are so lazy and stupid to blame our parents and the cupids," he wrote in another. He kept going back to the concepts of "tribe," "animal marking," and "territory," and those offshoots eventually evolved into a different song, "Territorial Pissings."

A few months prior, Kurt had written "Sliver," which he later described as his "most straightforward song." It paired the soft/loud technique with childish lyrics about a time he'd been left with his grandparents. "Mom and dad go off somewhere and leave the kid with his grandparents, and he gets confused and frightened; he doesn't understand what's happening to him," Kurt told *Melody Maker*. "But hey, you mustn't get too worried about him—grandpa doesn't abuse him or anything like that. And in the last verse, he wakes up back in his mother's arms." With his explanation, Kurt didn't sound like a songwriter describing a lyric; instead, he sounded like he was telling the story of his childhood.

As he began to imagine how the next record would be structured, he sorted the material into genders. "Sliver" was, not surprisingly, a "boy" song. Still thinking in the vinyl world of sides, he wanted one side to be "Boy" songs (with "Polly," "In Bloom," and a few others), and the other to be the "Girl" side, with his angry invectives of heartbreak. At another point, he took his song list and wrote emoticons next to the titles: "In Bloom" and "On a Plain" were happy; "Something in the Way" and "Polly" were sad; "Drain You" was "gross happy."

That August, the band finally went back on the road, hiring Dale Crover as their temporary drummer. Crover agreed to do the tour only if Kurt promised not to crash into his drums, warning Kurt that any transgression would be met with violence. Nirvana opened up for Sonic Youth on the two-week tour, which was tantamount to being selected as punk rock's runners-up. Nirvana lost money on the dates, but the opportunity for Kurt to get business advice from Sonic Youth's Thurston Moore was priceless. Eventually, Nirvana would hire Sonic Youth's management company and legal firm, and sign with their label, DGC.

A MONTH AFTER THE SONIC YOUTH DATES, Nirvana played a show at the Motor Sports International Garage in Seattle that drew 1,500 rabid fans; it was the band's only concert with Dan Peters on drums—Peters normally played with Mudhoney. Nirvana's next drummer—Dave Grohl—had flown in that very day for an audition and stood watching from the wings. More important than who the drummer was that night, the show marked a shift in how the press perceived Nirvana and how the band members perceived themselves. Now, a dozen labels were vying for the band's attention, wanting to purchase Sub Pop's interest. For years, Nirvana had played second fiddle to Mudhoney and the Melvins, but by this show, that equation was reversed. The Melvins were on the same bill, and it was clear to everyone—certainly to Buzz Osborne and Kurt Cobain—that the one-time student was now besting the mentor. It was as if, at that moment, on that very day, Nirvana arrived as a headlining band.

Kurt did several interviews before and after the show, and he sounded uncharacteristically confident about the future. "We figured we may as well get on the radio and try and make a little bit of money," Kurt told journalist Keith Cameron. "We're changing a little bit; we've been into more accessible pop styles of music." Interest from labels and radio made Kurt realize that his dream of living off his music just might work. He started to talk like a rock star for the first time, with a bravado that had previously been missing from his encounters with the press. The letters begging record companies to sign his band had ceased; now they were begging him. "I don't wanna have any other kind of job," he told Cameron. "I can't work among people. I may as well try and make a career out of this. All my life, my dream has been to be a big rock star—just may as well abuse it while you can." ■

ABOVE AND RIGHT September 22, 1990, at the Motor Sports International Garage show. Many felt this Seattle concert marked Nirvana's ascension to stardom. It also marked one of the first occasions the Melvins opened for Nirvana, reversing the roles the two bands had early on.

One can't appreciate the sea change that was *Nevermind* without grasping the state of the music industry in America as the nineties began. Vinyl albums were fading, compact discs were the latest sensation, and the tinny sound of the new format was perfect for the dominant music genre in 1990: lite-metal "hair bands." Rock radio in 1990 was dominated by power ballads from hair bands, like Bon Jovi's "Blaze of Glory" and Nelson's "Love and Affection." This latter song, a syrupy valentine by two blond twins, ranked as one of the year's biggest singles, and ironically, it came from the same label that would issue *Nevermind*. The other big hits of 1990 were by MC Hammer, Poison, Warrant, and Wilson Phillips.

Kurt Cobain had many creative gifts, but he may have been most skilled as a cultural critic. Writing about the state of music prior to the release of *Nevermind*, he succinctly surmised the dire state of rock 'n' roll pre-grunge. "Everything sucks," he wrote. "Too many compilations of present-day bands paying homage to old-influential bands." At twenty-three, Kurt already felt aged. "The younger generation never hardly heard old Aerosmith records, or Rod Stewart and the Small Faces, so they have no sense of plagiarism in the 'now' bands paying homage, supposedly, or keeping the faith. Six strings, twenty-four notes that repeat the same scale. . . . Rock 'n' roll: Thirty years equals exhausted!"

He wrote about current trends ("Hip hop/Rap? For the time being, yes, good, at least original; exhausted in three years"); corporate ownership of radio ("play it safe; what sells"); and feminist politics ("probably some ideas left in an unsaturated vagina"). He ended this particular analysis with the best financial advice that could be offered in 1991, the start of a long advance in America's housing market: "Get into real estate!"

That last remake might have been the result of Kurt's own consideration of real estate investment around the start of 1991. He had no money, as his DGC deal wouldn't close until April, and most of that advance would go toward recording costs, but he couldn't help conjecturing how he

RIGHT Los Angeles, California, May 1991. Michael Lavine shot this photo as part of the album sessions for *Nevermind*. Finally finished with recording, the band was more playful than usual.

ABOVE Kurt writing in his journal backstage in Amsterdam, November 1991.

might live when he was rich. He called an Olympia real estate agent and picked up a list of available properties. He wasn't looking at single-family dwellings; he wanted to buy a commercial structure to build a recording studio and living space. He got as far as touring a few properties, but he never made an offer since he was still having trouble paying the rent on his tiny flat.

Though Nirvana was being written about as the next big thing—particularly in the U.K.—good press didn't buy groceries. The band had spent the fall being wined and dined by label executives, but once they signed with DGC, they could no longer eat out on record-label expense accounts. Their opportunities to tour were limited, as they expected any week to go into the studio—though the new album session was delayed repeatedly. Dave Grohl was living with Kurt and sleeping on his four-and-a-half-foot-long sofa—which was a foot and a half shorter than Grohl. Grohl was in an Olympia laundromat one day when a Nirvana fan recognized him from a previous show and asked why a star didn't have someone to do those kinds of errands for him.

That winter, waiting for the label money to come and with no girlfriend to support him, Kurt was poorer than he'd ever been. For a time, he had to pawn his belongings, including his amplifier, until a tiny overseas royalty payment arrived. Kurt and Dave ate only corn dogs, pizza, Fruity Pebbles cereal, and Kraft macaroni and cheese. The apartment had always been filled with Kurt's collectibles; now dozens of used pizza boxes added to the clutter. Grohl told one journalist it was a mess, "just fucking demolished, an absolute fucking Dumpster."

RIGHT In Kurt's diverse collection of pop culture debris, he also had a number of Jim Crow-era collectibles, including this porcelain doll. It was the kitsch aspect that attracted Kurt to these items; he was always stridently anti-racist, and he performed at several anti-hate benefits. On an occasion when a famous rock star insulted a bandmate with a racial slur, Kurt told the star to fuck off.

Finally, Nirvana's new management stepped in and started sending Kurt $1,000 a month as an advance. Kurt immediately bought a 1963 Plymouth Valiant for $500. It already had 140,000 miles on it, but he adored it nonetheless. He also bought a secondhand television, which was used more than the car. A little later that spring, a check for $3,000 arrived from a publishing deal. Kurt spent over a third of that check at Toys "R" Us buying a video game system, two realistic-looking BB guns, and dozens of action figures. He also purchased two PixelVision video cameras and used these to start filming the band—some of his footage would later be used in the official release *Live! Tonight! Sold Out!!* Filming with his video camera became his current creative obsession, and his art projects in other mediums were moved to the back burner.

Several months went by while Kurt waited for the call that would announce the start of the recording session. He used his new car to drive to the ocean or to Aberdeen, and once he went to watch a demolition derby. Until Grohl moved out that spring, the two celebrated an extended adolescence, shooting out windows with their BB guns and putting plastic dog feces on chairs before visitors sat down. Dave taught Kurt how to make homemade tattoos, and Kurt later had the K Records logo put on his arm.

Even as Kurt was planning how to spend his DGC advance, he was still talking about signing with indie label K instead. It was mostly talk, since Kurt never actually approached K directly. In all likelihood, the idea that he could sign with an indie made Kurt feel less guilty about

TOP LEFT Not only did Kurt use Milk of Magnesia, Tums, Maalox, and various other over-the-counter medicines for his stomach problems, but he also collected antique boxes of such remedies.

BOTTOM LEFT Kurt and Dave Grohl during a smoke break on tour.

BELOW Kurt with Sonic Youth's Thurston Moore, who was both idol and mentor to Kurt. Nirvana eventually signed with Sonic Youth's record label, management company, booking agent, and law firm.

inking a deal with a major, so it was a useful fantasy. Still, it must have been odd for executives at DGC to read Kurt's interviews—after he'd signed the pricey DGC deal—and to hear their latest musical hope talk about how he wanted to be on an indie label. When, finally, the call came that the sessions would start in May, Kurt hastily gathered his notebooks full of lyrics and headed for Los Angeles.

THE SINGLE MOST TELLING BIT OF TRIVIA about the *Nevermind* sessions, which took place at Sound City Studios in Van Nuys, California, was that the hair band Warrant preceded Nirvana in the facility. Warrant was huge at the time, while Nirvana was unknown. One night, Kurt grabbed the in-studio address system and screamed, "Bring me some 'Cherry Pie,'" a reference to Warrant's last big hit. Other than that, the two groups did not cross paths.

Butch Vig had been selected to produce Nirvana's album, giving him a chance to complete what he'd begun a year earlier with the 1990 Smart session. The recording sessions were relatively uneventful, though Kurt hadn't yet completed his lyrics, which meant that the rest of the band often sat around waiting. "We were just standing there with our arms crossed and our feet tapping, just staring at Kurt as he sat there sweating, and writing, and looking, and writing, and looking," Novoselic told *The Rocket*. Kurt had been working on some of the songs for as long as three years, but he couldn't resist the urge to tinker with them one last time.

When they weren't at the studio, the band hung out at Venice Beach and partied. At the time, Kurt was not the wildest member of the band; that honor fell to Novoselic, who was once pulled over for drunk driving. The band was staying in a long-term rental in an apartment complex, and, as was typical of nearly everywhere he lived, Kurt wrote graffiti on the walls. When the band finally left, the record label was stuck with a huge bill for damages.

After three weeks of recording, the album was nearly complete, and the band turned their attention to the album cover and a music video, both of which Kurt had meticulously planned. While DGC was open to Kurt's ideas, the label was not willing to let him direct the band's first professional music video by himself, no matter how much he protested. Consequently, the video shoot for "Smells Like Teen Spirit" was more difficult for Kurt than any other element of the album preparation. He had sketched out several ideas in his notebook for what he wanted to be "a pep rally from hell." He needed: "Mercedes-Benz and a few old cars; access to abandoned mall, main floor and one jewelry shop; lots of fake jewelry; school auditorium (gym); a cast of hundreds, one custodian, students; and six black cheerleader outfits with Anarchy 'A's on chest." Kurt's initial video concept had the school janitor as the central figure. Kurt never told the video director, or anyone else involved in the production, that he himself had been a janitor at his own high school.

The label had hired Sam Bayer to direct, and considering Kurt's jealousy, it's no surprise that Kurt later called Bayer a "little Napoleon." The director used a bullhorn to corral the extras—many of whom had been recruited at a Nirvana show at the Roxy, so they were true fans. Bayer wanted the crowd to look bored during the beginning of the song, to act mildly interested in the middle section, and to jump around toward the end. What he got instead was a group of fans who went wild the instant filming began. "The crowd was completely out of control, and the director was screaming at the top of his lungs for everyone to fucking calm down and be cool, or they'll get kicked out," Dave Grohl told *Newsweek*. "It was pretty hilarious, actually, seeing this man trying to control these children who just wanted to destroy." Though a smoke machine was used during the shoot, most of what looked like haze in the final video edit was chalk dust from stage marks on the floor that were being trampled by the rabid crowd.

Kurt had always been enormously self-conscious about the fact that he was skinny, so for the video shoot, he wore several layers of clothes; he was also concerned about an acne breakout. He wore the same clothes he wore every day: Levi's 501 jeans, a long underwear shirt, and black Converse Chuck Taylor sneakers. The final video may have been far from what Kurt had planned, but it did prove one undeniable fact: Even with multiple layers of clothes, Kurt was extremely pho-togenic. He had star power in front of the camera, and even his odd fashion choices soon became

RIGHT Kurt's favorite pair of Converse sneakers. He has written "ENDORSEMENT" on the right toe cap.

...e of the biggest
...f the most
...und rock scene.

...d their first
...g. An
... *Nevermind* is an
...ntful, compelling...

...e and beautiful

..it" and two
...nd "Aneurysm."

...eveland, OH
...etroit, MI
...icago, IL
...nneapolis, MN
... Louis, MO
...wrence, KS
...llas, TX
...ouston, TX
...stin, TX
...oenix, AZ
...uana, Mexico
...s Angeles, CA
...n Francisco, CA
...rtland, OR
...ncouver, B.C.
...attle, WA

trendy. Several months later, when his choice in footwear single-handedly reinvigorated sales of Converse sneakers, he jokingly wrote the word "ENDORSEMENT" on the rubber toe cap of his Chuck Taylors.

IT WASN'T UNTIL EARLY JUNE, after the Sound City sessions had wrapped up, that Kurt came upon a title for the album. He had finally given up on *Sheep* and decided that a more ironic moniker would do, and that it would be *Nevermind*, a line from "Smells Like Teen Spirit." The fact that the name was grammatically incorrect was a bonus for Kurt, and it also paid homage to the Sex Pistols' album *Never Mind the Bollocks*. With one word, Kurt could name-check the most famous punk album and prove himself less grammatically correct than the Pistols.

When it came to the cover, the label was more open to Kurt's input. Kurt wanted the cover to feature a picture of a woman giving birth underwater, captured at the point the baby's head began to exit the vagina. During one of his late-night television jags, he had seen a program about underwater birthing centers, and the topic fascinated him. The more gory and bloody the photo, Kurt argued, the better. He was convinced this explicit image would help sell his band to the masses. The label was unable to clear rights to the birthing program, so another idea of Kurt's, one that involved fewer bodily fluids, was pursued: showing a picture of a baby underwater, chasing a dollar bill.

A stock photo was first considered, but when that also proved too costly, photographer Kirk Weddle shot pictures of several babies, both boys and girls, swimming underwater. The initial sketch didn't call for the baby's penis to be visible, but in the end, the photo that was clearest happened to be a boy with a protruding penis. Given Kurt's fascination with female genitalia, it seems surprising, in retrospect, that he did not insist on having a vagina on the back cover. As it was, the back cover did include an anatomy lesson of sorts: a picture of the vagina/meat collage once pasted to Kurt's refrigerator. In the middle of the collage was Kurt's favorite monkey, Chim-Chim. This personal touch gave unknowing buyers a tiny peek into Kurt's Olympia apartment.

Once the album was complete, the band took off on a glorious jaunt through Europe, once again playing with Sonic Youth. All three members of Nirvana would later recall this period as their most joyful. While there was anticipation for the upcoming release, there was little pressure or obligation, and the tour was a time of food fights, boyish pranks, and legendary performances, like the Reading Festival show—still talked about as one of Nirvana's greatest live moments.

When the tour ended, Kurt returned to his Olympia apartment to discover all his stuff—his glorious collection of oddities—sitting in boxes on the curb or in the garage. He had been evicted for failing to pay the rent while he was on tour. Not knowing what else to do, he slept curled up in the backseat of his car, with his precious Chuck Taylors still on his feet. ∎

LEFT Promotional stickers from DGC were a big step forward from Kurt's homemade labels. DGC was unsure if the album would do well, so a number of promotional items and ads, such as the ones shown here, were made up in the early fall of 1991. They were sent to radio stations, newspapers, and clubs. As it turned out, the promotional efforts were hardly necessary—the album sold beyond all expectations.

7. — NEVERMIND TRISKAIDEKAPHOBIA

evermind was released on September 24, 1991. Despite later stories to the contrary, it was not an out-of-the-box runaway smash. It did, however, sell beyond the label's expectations, which initially called for a run of only 40,000 copies. They doubled that order just as the album shipped, but even that greater supply fell short, and when record stores ran out of stock, the album's chart progress was temporarily stalled. It debuted in *Billboard* at Number 34, impressive for a major-label debut, but not as high as Mudhoney's last album had placed. It would take almost three months before the album would top the charts in a slow but steady rise.

Still, in some pockets of the country, the single was all over the radio, and the video was constantly on MTV. Though radio play certainly helped make *Nevermind* a hit, the "Smells Like Teen Spirit" video may have played the leading role in bringing Nirvana to the consciousness of Middle America. Kurt had been angry at the director, who had ignored his ideas during the shoot; now his irate-yet-handsome image was all over television.

The band was already on tour when the album was released, but they had held their official record release party earlier in September at the Re-bar in Seattle. It was Friday the thirteenth, and in a play on the date, the invitations read, "Nevermind Triskaidekaphobia, here's Nirvana." Kurt had originally wanted the party at the Java Jive in Tacoma, a landmark tavern shaped like a teapot. The tavern, which smelled a bit like Kurt's apartment since two chimpanzees were on display, was one of Kurt's favorite hangouts. The Java Jive idea was abandoned when the label decided that holding a party thirty miles from Seattle—where most of the state's music businesses were based—might not be the best idea.

Yet Kurt's initial choice of location said much about Nirvana's evolving relationship with Seattle, the Northwest's biggest city. Despite the fact that the media would inevitably list the group as part of the "Seattle Sound," Nirvana was always more of an Aberdeen, Olympia, or Tacoma band. At the time *Nevermind* was released in 1991, Dave Grohl was the only band member living in Seattle (and even he had just moved there after he grew sick of Kurt's sofa). Novoselic lived in Tacoma, and

RIGHT Kurt often wore multiple layers of clothes, both to keep himself warm and to appear less skinny. For this photo session in London, Kurt is wearing two T-shirts, two pair of jeans, a sweater, an overcoat, a leather jacket, and a pair of fingerless gloves.

Kurt still lived in his car in Olympia or crashed with friends. It would not be until the band grew rich off *Nevermind* that all three members would finally move to Seattle, years after the media had initially defined them as a Seattle band.

The band pointed out as much in its interviews, but few in the media bothered to explain the geographical or cultural differences between Aberdeen and Seattle. As Nirvana made its way across North America in the fall of 1991, the press had far juicier topics to cover than the band's zip code. Kurt and Krist were both outrageous interview subjects (Grohl was less media savvy and less weird), and wherever the band went, they made good copy.

Over the course of two months, they did several dozen interviews and attempted to reframe their success at the same time that they were enjoying it. They insulted both DGC and Sub Pop frequently, even as DGC reps picked them up and drove them to their interviews. "They have people who work there who don't even like music," Kurt told *Melody Maker* of his label. As for their former drummers, Kurt announced, "We're sick and tired of working with lame idiots." His writing technique, he explained to Toronto's *Meat* fanzine, came from "a lot of notebooks that I can just use as reference. I can take lines out of things that were written before when I write poetry and stuff like that." This last part was true, as whenever Kurt was stumped to come up with a line for a new song, he simply whipped out his trusty journals and plucked out a previously written couplet.

As the album climbed the charts and became a smash, Kurt increased his diatribes against MTV and the society that was embracing him. "One of the most important diseases that we're against is gluttony, consumerism and that kind of stuff," he told one interviewer. Meanwhile, he phoned almost every day to check the chart progress of the album and the status of his video.

And after critics began to relabel *Nevermind* a pop record rather than a punk one, Kurt himself embraced the shift by simply explaining that all the punk he'd touted for so long was actually pop. "People in the underground have denied pop for the last few years," he told *New Route*. "I don't understand that at all, because the Ramones were pop. The Sex Pistols were pop. So were the Clash and a lot of other bands. Fucking Black Flag is pop in a way." He echoed the same thought to *Hit Parader*: "We've always liked some pop music, even if it wasn't very commercial." Perhaps the most interesting nugget in the autumn 1991 interviews was Kurt's mentioning that he already had enough new material to record another album, which he said he hoped to do quickly.

Yet as the success of the album grew beyond even Kurt's wildest expectations, the label discouraged talk of another record, so as not to compete with *Nevermind*. The conventional wisdom in the record industry was never to release a new album if your last one was still in the top ten. As *Nevermind* continued to pass sales marks once thought impossible—first gold-record status and then platinum before the end of the year—Kurt grew timid.

OUTSIDE FLAP Kurt's acoustic guitar case. The sticker in the center is for Poison Idea, a Portland, Oregon, punk band that was a contemporary of Nirvana.

INSIDE FLAP (Left) The Epiphone acoustic with the "Nixon Now" sticker is a model called the Texan. Kurt purchased this from a Los Angeles guitar shop after he became famous. Kurt's guitar tech, Earnie Bailey, installed the Bartolini 3AV pickup. (Center) Kurt signed an endorsement deal with Fender in 1992, and the company began to provide him with the occasional free guitar. This blue Mustang was one of three that Fender sent Kurt just prior to the *In Utero* tour. The humbucking pickup and modifications to the bridge were done by Earnie Bailey in 1993, and the switch tips were removed by Jim Vincent in early 1994. Other modifications included changing the bridge pickup to a black Seymour Duncan JB (Jeff Beck) model, and the bridge was changed to a Gotoh Tune-o-matic. Finally, the tailpiece had the springs removed to disable the vibrato, and washers were added to better keep it in tune. (Right) Earnie Bailey purchased this sunburst Univox Hi-Flier for Kurt in 1993.

The fall *Nevermind* tour had been booked into small clubs, and there were overflow crowds. The band would drive up to a sold-out venue only to find an extra thousand kids waiting outside. "Back then Mudhoney was like the glass ceiling," recalled Blackie Onassis, whose band Urge Overkill opened for Nirvana on that tour. "Kurt was always talking about this, how the 100,000 level was it, and that none of the bands had sold more than that. But they blew over that line, and the tour was nuts."

Before the shows, Kurt would spend his free time doodling in his journals. Onassis remembered Kurt showing off a number of his cartoons and enjoying a copy of the Dan Clowes comic *Eightball,* which Onassis had loaned him. "Kurt loved Clowes's style," Onassis said. "He talked quite a bit about drawing. He reminded me of this hesher-kid who was always scribbling in a notebook. His drawings to me looked like small-town pot smoker stuff." Kurt's notebook, as it had been for years, was filled with images of aliens, puppets, and dismembered carcasses.

When Kurt deemed it necessary to talk to the press, they continued to hover around his every word, but his time as a cooperative subject was quickly passing. At one show, Kurt ignored the major newspaper critics and instead spent his time debating a fanzine writer who had committed the crime of describing Nirvana as a "heavy metal band." "He seemed more concerned about what the fanzines wrote about him," Onassis recalled. "He felt it was his need to point out to writers the nuances of the punk rock scene pre-Nirvana." In an interview with *Kerrang,* Kurt complained that most writers ignored his history lessons and only wanted dirt: "I've talked for hours with journalists about being in rock 'n' roll and it never gets printed."

As the tour continued, and the shows sold out at an even more rapid pace, there was a tone of something like embarrassment in some of the interviews Kurt did. "It's becoming a bit exaggerated," he told *RIP.* "I'm looking forward to some backlash, at least in criticism, because there's so much anticipation, so much encouragement by our friends and our label, that I'm afraid."

"People have called our record perfect," Novoselic added. "That's bad."

BY EARLY 1992, most journalists who were sent to interview Nirvana found that they were now facing off against only Krist and Dave. Kurt often was reported as ill on interview days; only for cover stories would he talk to the press now. Dave and Krist said roughly the same things Kurt did, railing against corporations and recounting humorous touring stories, but sometimes their insights into Kurt were even more telling than his own. "I lived with Kurt for eight months," Dave told *Rolling Stone.* "When I first got there, he had just broken up with a girl and was totally heartbroken. We would sit in this tiny, shoebox apartment for eight hours at a time without saying a word. For weeks and weeks this happened. Finally, one night, we were driving back in the van, and Kurt said, 'You know, I'm not always like this.'"

RIGHT In Nirvana's early days, the band's only gimmick was Kurt's habit of playing guitar solos while lying on his back onstage. Even when the band became famous and tricks were no longer necessary, he occasionally did a solo this way.

TOP LEFT Kurt and Carrie Montgomery in a rare lighthearted moment on tour. Montgomery was Mark Arm's girlfriend and became one of Kurt's few platonic female friends.

CENTER LEFT Kurt backstage with Mark Arm and Dan Peters of Mudhoney. Peters had played one show as Nirvana's drummer.

BOTTOM LEFT Arm and Cobain in a photo taken by Courtney Love, shown in the mirror's reflection.

When Dave was asked if the band's success was overwhelming, he gave an answer that would say much about his future plans: "I just don't want to be David Grohl of Nirvana for the rest of my life. It's like the kid who got caught masturbating in the bathroom of the high school. That's the only way he's ever known."

Kurt's mental and physical challenges seemed to grow in direct correlation to his fame. As the band's audiences increased, so did his stomach pain and depression. Outwardly, his career was taking off, but neither fame nor money seemed to make him any happier. He had sought attention and recognition for his art his entire life, but when he finally achieved those goals through music, to a degree beyond his wildest dreams, he found them hollow. The success of the band also came with something for which Kurt hadn't planned: There were now huge expectations on him from the label, his band members, the press, and himself.

Kurt had used drugs since age fifteen as a way to blot out his feelings, but few describe pre-fame behavior that could be classified as addictlike. He had tried marijuana, alcohol, LSD, speed, and a few other drugs, but none had been used excessively. He had started smoking cigarettes in high school, but stopped after he formed the band, thinking it harmed his voice, and didn't start up again until 1990. He rarely drank, arguing that alcohol hurt his stomach.

Heroin, however, was another matter. His journals provide a remarkable catalog of his drug history. In them, Kurt confesses to having used heroin—which he calls "heroine," personifying the drug—in Aberdeen as early as 1987, and then using it "ten more times from '87 to '90." Strangely, none of Kurt's Aberdeen friends recall heroin being a drug that Kurt, in his abject poverty, could afford. But it is possible that he was considering any opiate, even in pill form, as heroin, and certainly as a teen he had used narcotic cough syrups. By the time Kurt moved to Olympia in 1988, he was occasionally injecting heroin on drug binges. In his journal entry, he directly correlated his drug usage to his stomach ailments: "The only thing that I found that worked were heavy opiates." He admitted his decision to use heroin was a "choice," though one that he connected directly to the demands of touring: "After the last European tour, I vowed to never go on tour again unless my condition is either masked or cured."

As 1991 wound down, and Nirvana was still on tour with no end in sight, an unfortunate series of circumstances coalesced to create a storm of controversy. Kurt visited various doctors in numerous cities, seeking help for his ever-increasing stomach problems, to no avail. To self-medicate, he increased his drug usage to a point where he began to nod off in interviews. He was now the biggest rock star in the world, and his every move was of interest to the press. When one journalist hinted at Kurt's stoned-like behavior during an interview, it unleashed a torrent of attention from the rest of the press. Suddenly, Kurt's drug problems became as talked about as the band's music.

ABOVE In early 1992, Nirvana did a tour of Australia and Japan, where they were hugely popular. At the Tokyo airport customs gate, Kurt found it humorous to have Courtney photograph him in front of pictures of illegal drugs.

FOLLOWING LEFT Kurt in Japan in 1992. Of all religions, he felt most comfortable with Buddhism, and would chant and meditate at times. He became fascinated by Jain Dharma, an Indian philosophy that emphasized respect for all living things. The Jain philosophy of worshipping even small animals fit with Kurt's fascination with animals.

FOLLOWING RIGHT Kurt in Japan.

To Kurt, the singular focus seemed hypocritical. There were dozens of drug addicts in alternative rock, and some were profiled alongside Nirvana in stories about the Seattle scene, but it seemed like only his problems were of interest to the press. Kurt's bandmates were no saints, and many in the greater Nirvana camp regularly used drugs or alcohol. Now that the band was huge, and so much was riding on him to lead it, Kurt rebelled. "They're not going to be able to tell me to stop," he later told Michael Azerrad about his band. "So I really didn't care. Obviously to them it was like practicing witchcraft or something. They didn't know anything about it so they thought that any second, I was going to die."

Kurt didn't die that fall, but he came close. When the band headlined *Saturday Night Live* on January 12, 1992, it was also, remarkably, the first time he overdosed. He was revived at the last moment—a pattern that would become common. Over the next two years, Kurt's addiction became a shroud over his life, defusing the great successes but also clouding the defeats. There would be many more overdoses, several attempts at rehab, and many heartbreaking struggles ahead.

KURT'S DRUG PROBLEM MAY HAVE CAUSED HIM TO NOD OUT during an occasional interview, but he finished the grueling U.S. tour, and the shows themselves were tremendous. The final tour dates were perhaps the biggest challenge, as Nirvana was the opener on a bill with Pearl Jam and the Red Hot Chili Peppers. These shows had been contracted long before Nirvana's rise to fame and were just one example of how the band's success overran their ability to plan.

Despite Kurt's personal struggles, his artistic life continued to thrive, his sense of humor remained intact, and his strong intellect was unmarred. He kept writing songs at a frantic pace, and the band performed over seventy-five shows in the four months that followed the release of *Nevermind*. He continued to sketch in his notebook, though there wasn't much time for full-on art projects. He continued to play with his video camera, using it both to capture the band on the road and to film home movies of his personal life.

Photography had never interested Kurt as much as painting, but in 1991 he bought both a Polaroid and a film camera and used them to document the mad life that had become his world. With his Polaroid, he would often shoot a picture and then use a cotton swab to smear the emulsion before it set, creating miniature paintings out of the images.

One of the first places he turned the camera's lens was on his new girlfriend, Courtney Love. He had met Courtney on the road earlier in his career, and by the fall 1991 *Nevermind* tour, they were not just dating but seemingly bonded for life. She jokingly told one reporter that it was "pharmaceuticals" that brought them together, and on one date that was true—both took swings from a bottle of codeine cough syrup. Their attraction to each other, however, was deeper than that quip

FLAP A promotional postcard sent out to attract attention to Nirvana's first appearance on *Saturday Night Live* in January 1992. The next week *Nevermind* knocked Michael Jackson out of the top spot on the *Billboard* sales charts. The tagline "turns your T.V. into a boxful of bliss" was written by a DGC marketing rep, but to any longtime Nirvana fan it had some hidden significance—Bliss was one of the names the band played under before they settled on Nirvana.

OPPOSITE As Nirvana's fame mushroomed, Kurt found less time to write in his diary. Despite his growing wealth and stature, many of the entries he did write continued to reflect self-doubt.

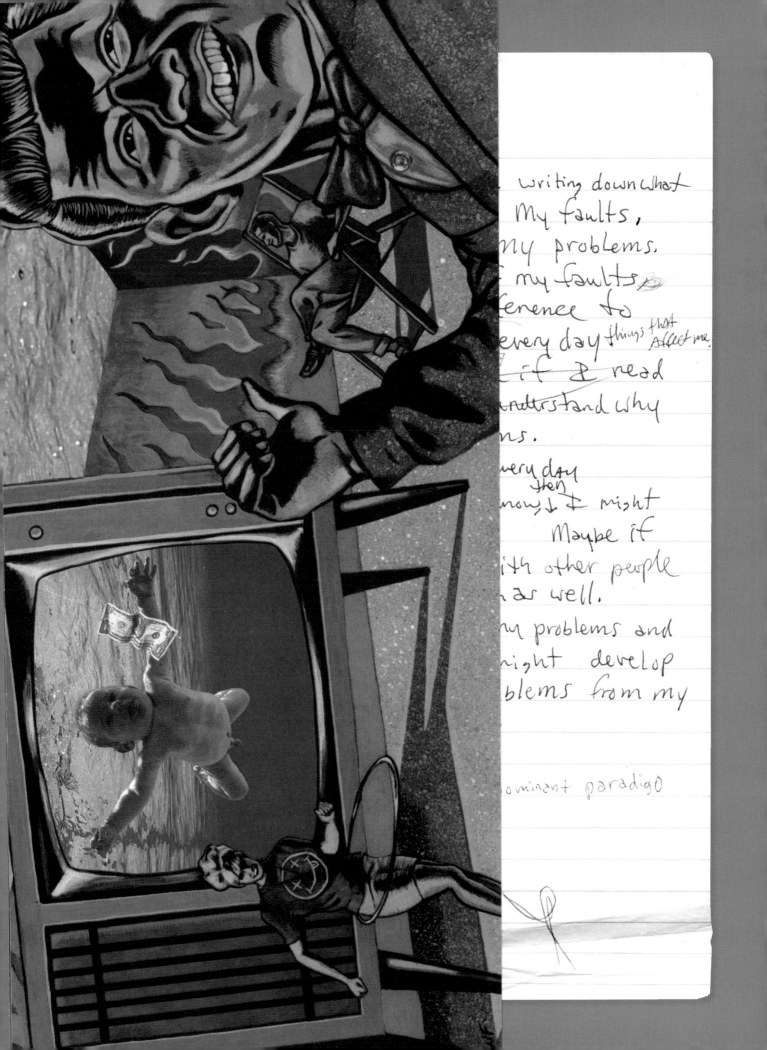

writing down what
My faults,
my problems.
my faults
erence to
every day things that affect me.
if I read
understand why
ns.

very day
then
now, I might
Maybe if
ith other people
as well.

ny problems and
might develop
blems from my

ominant paradigO

ABOVE October 4, 1992, Seattle, Washington. Nirvana did a surprise show at the Crocodile Cafe, opening up for Mudhoney. They were billed as "Pen Cap Chew," an early name Kurt had considered for the band, and performed an hour-long set. At one point, Kurt asked the audience for requests, and Krist Novoselic yelled into the microphone, "Play 'Teen Spirit.'" They didn't play that song, or any of their other hits. During Mudhoney's portion of the show, Kurt came back onstage and dived into the audience. The crowd caught him.

indicated. It was also much more than their obvious sexual bond, made clear by the number of nude pictures Kurt took of Courtney.

When Kurt had first moved to Olympia, he railed against class differences but found himself hanging out with middle- or upper-class Evergreen State College students, none of whom had grown up as poor as he had. Most of his girlfriends hadn't known the kinds of struggles he'd gone through in his youth, when he was forced to live in dozens of different homes, surviving hand to mouth. Courtney's childhood, in contrast, was as fractured and tragic as Kurt's. Both had been so poor that they had gotten food stamps; both had struggled to find a single positive adult role model; and both believed that one day they could escape their circumstances through their art. That they also each showed signs of narcissism was no surprise, considering the neglect they grew up with. Each saw in the other the pre-damaged innocent child, and it was a youthful, familial connection they expressed when describing their union. They were almost too much alike, and consequently they also shared many of the same demons, including drugs.

It was their mutual struggle with addiction that journalists immediately focused in on, but those portraits failed to include their intellectual connection or the dry, ghoulish humor they shared. While there is no denying that Courtney pursued Kurt and literally flew around the world chasing

ABOVE Kurt took this photograph of a heart-shaped box he had positioned on top of some sheets of aluminum.

him, he was equally smitten with her. He sent her a series of faxes, notes, bouquets, and cartoons that fall, which were intended to woo her. "I am eternally grateful for your priceless opinions and advice," read one. "I am forever indebted. I am not worth [enough] to be in the presence of you. And I will walk ten steps behind with my head hung in shame, infested with guilt for having the privilege to ever have met my eyes with yours and to be blessed with your solace and wisdom." A line from this note would later end up in "Heart-Shaped Box."

Courtney was a brash, assertive woman who did not suffer fools gladly. That she was immediately disliked by Kurt's managers came as no surprise, because he listened to her advice above that of others. Many of Kurt's associates worried that she would enable his drug use, but criticism only seemed to ignite Kurt's protectiveness of her, perhaps because Courtney was so much like him. In one note to her that also summed up his own personality, he wrote: "I think it's pathetic that the entire world looks upon a person with patience and a calm demeanor, as the desired model-citizen. Yet there's something to be said about the ability to explain one's self with a toned down tune deaf tone."

The same entry continued on as an ode of a sort: "How I metamorphosized from hyperactive to cement is, for lack of a better knife to the throat, uh, annoying, aggravating, confusing, as dense as cement. Cement holds no other minerals. You can't even find fool's gold in it. It's strictly man-made, and you've taught me it's okay to be a man, and in the classic man's world. I parade around you proudly like the ring on my finger, which also holds no mineral. Love, Kurt."

Despite her toughness, Courtney was also a girlie girl, and she encouraged Kurt, perhaps for the first time in his life, to assert his machismo. He had always been fascinated by gender roles, and occasionally even dressed in women's clothes, but Courtney encouraged him to play up his maleness, even if he was wearing eyeliner. ∎

ABOVE Kurt with his half sister, Brianne. He adored her, as he did all children.

TOP RIGHT Kurt and Courtney in Europe during the fall of 1991.

BOTTOM RIGHT Kurt and Courtney during Christmas of 1991 in Kurt's mother's home in Aberdeen, Washington, where Kurt had taken Courtney to meet his family. On the table to the left is a photo of Kurt's sister, Kim.

8

BEST DRUG

Late in the fall of 1991, Courtney became pregnant. In February 1992, she and Kurt married on a beach in Honolulu, Hawaii, and in the spring the couple moved to Los Angeles, California. It was the first and only time Kurt lived anywhere outside of Washington State. At the height of his fame, he made a decision to put Nirvana on hold and turn down lucrative offers to tour. In lieu of the band, he picked up a paintbrush and contemplated a life without music. "I just got up and got drugs and listened to music and painted and played the guitar. That's about it," Kurt told Michael Azerrad. It was both a retreat from the music business and an embracing of his artistic muse.

The couple had moved into a two-bedroom stucco apartment they rented for $1,100 a month. It was on Spaulding Avenue in the Fairfax District—not the kind of locale in which many would expect to find the world's most famous rock star. The apartment was near Canter's Delicatessen, and Kurt sometimes ate a late breakfast there in the afternoon with sunglasses on. Few imagined that the disheveled man in the corner was the one who had launched the grunge revolution and who was still all over MTV. In Los Angeles, a city full of movie stars, Kurt found an anonymity that couldn't be had elsewhere.

Kurt lost his driver's license over unpaid traffic tickets, and Courtney had never learned how to drive, so they relied on taxis. Kurt could also occasionally be seen walking up Melrose, shuffling along with a walk that looked like that of a senior citizen. Due to his back problems, he had developed a distinct gait that made him look much older than he was. He wore long raincoats even on sunny days, giving him the look of an eccentric or a mad scientist.

And for several months, he was ensconced in a mad world of creation. He continued writing songs, and he later said that he crafted most of *In Utero* during these few months of retreat. But most days he was more focused on visual arts than on his rock-star career. He painted using acrylics and oils, but at times he mixed his own blood, semen, cigarette ash, and fecal matter into his medium. Almost no one saw what he created, since only a few people even knew where they

RIGHT Kurt in the living room of his Los Angeles apartment on Spaulding Avenue, spring 1992. As Nirvana's commercial impact grew during that year, Def Leppard would be on far fewer magazine covers.

lived, and Kurt rarely ventured out. He often would paint cartoons directly onto the walls, and he graffitied them as he had in his other homes. That spring, the word "patricide" was written in large letters on their living room wall.

Earlier in his life, Kurt couldn't afford oil paint or even canvases, but now he bought fine oils, quality brushes, and dozens of canvases, and set up an easel in the living room. In the summer of 1992, Kurt's childhood friend Jesse Reed came down from Aberdeen and found a working artist's studio in the Spaulding apartment. "He said he was getting out of music and he was taking painting seriously," Reed recalled. "He had six easels, and everything was full; there were eight paintings there. He was doing three a day, he told me." Kurt mentioned to Jesse that he was thinking of opening his own gallery.

There was a primitivism to Kurt's style, though each painting had at its core a substantial presence. One painting had a modernistic bright orange background and a diseased dog tooth hanging from the center of the canvas on a string. Another showed an alien on puppet strings with a miniature shriveled penis; a small cat peered in from the corner looking like something from a Lewis Carroll story. Another canvas featured a different puppetlike figure, lounging in a purple netherworld with a seahorse on his knee. Yet another featured red paint splotches that were arranged like a Rorschach test; dried flowers were affixed to the middle.

Many of the creations were multidimensional and had bits of plants, soil, newspaper clippings, broken porcelain doll parts, or human hair adhered to them. The themes were death, birth, menstruation, sexuality, heaven, and hell. Ghosts hid behind crosses; images of Satan sported huge erect penises; seahorses or eunuchlike figures peered out from the shadows. Kurt's stomach ailment also became part of the inspiration, and he told friends some paintings were his attempt to visualize the pain. Others were drug-related: They were his effort to capture on canvas the ecstasy and escape of getting high.

ABOVE LEFT Kurt in the Spaulding Avenue apartment, posing with a friend's parrot. Though the walls of the apartment were covered with graffiti, Kurt and Courtney had added the large "Gerard Cosloy" slogan for the benefit of a *Newsweek* photo session. Cosloy was the co-founder of Matador Records and worked with influential Homestead Records, two labels that Kurt would have preferred to the one he was signed to.

ABOVE Writing in his diary in his Los Angeles apartment.

FLAP Kurt loved porcelain doll heads, and he frequently repainted them or added touches like human hair or teeth. He used white and pink paint to retouch this particular doll. The green spot on the eyebrow is a chip in the porcelain.

OPPOSITE Kurt wrote on anything and everything that came across his path, including the back of his smashed guitar.

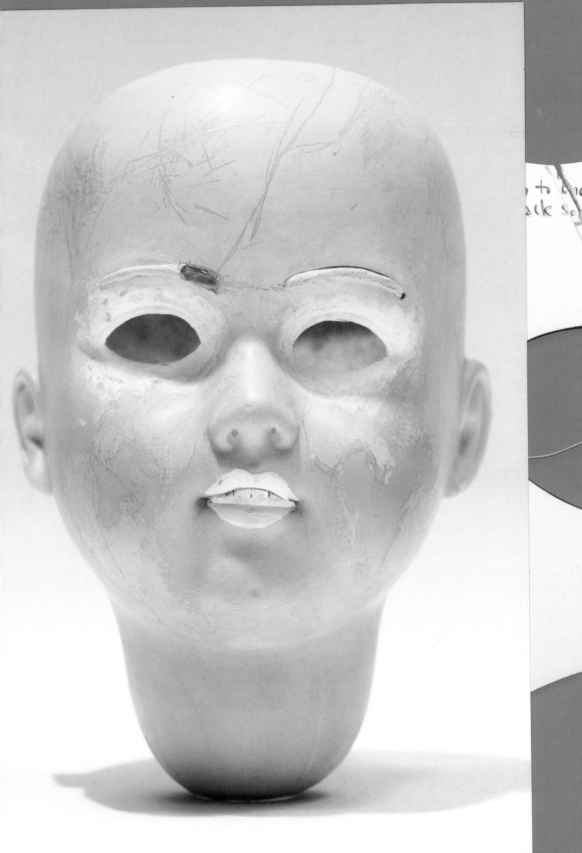

to know that you'll
ack someday

All
Are

At one point, he had so many works in progress that parts of the house had to be partitioned off. "He would store piles of stuff against the walls," recalled Rene Navarette, who worked as an on-call assistant for the couple. "We'd have to rope off these paintings. He was insecure about his talents, but he was definitely driven. It wasn't something that he talked about a lot, and many of the projects went unfinished."

One of his neighbors recalled Kurt mentioning the work of David Hockney as an inspiration. Some of Kurt's work had a Jackson Pollock look as he dripped candle wax on to the canvas or threw paint from a foot away. There was no single dominant style, though most owed much to surrealism and abstract expressionism, with doe-eyed figures peeking out from corners. As he had earlier, he also altered thrift store paintings by contributing his own slogans or additions. To one straightforward landscape he'd bought at a corner store, he added the word "Kurtisan" to the image, a play on the phrase "Kurt is insane."

For the first time since high school, music was now secondary to art for Kurt. When his Nirvana bandmates stopped by to talk business, they were shocked that he'd gotten so serious about something other than the band. "He was truly very talented," Krist Novoselic recalled. "If you look at his drawings, and the stuff that he did even as far back as high school, it was really good. He was an artist, really, in every sense of the word. In every village there's a carpenter and a blacksmith. Well, Kurt, he was the village artist."

Novoselic and Grohl, however, wondered whether there was room for a village artist in Nirvana. For the first of many times, Kurt began to talk of breaking up the band. "Kurt was in his own world at that point," Novoselic added. "After that, I was pretty estranged [from] him. It was never the same. We talked about the direction of the band somewhat, but there really was *no* direction of the band after that."

DRUGS WERE AS INTEGRAL A PART OF KURT'S LIFE that spring as his creativity was. He was using as often as twice a day and spending as much as $400 a day on heroin, though that figure, touted by Kurt, was surely inflated, as dealers routinely overcharged him. To anyone who witnessed his retreat into addiction, he never appeared high, strangely. It was as if heroin no longer made him euphoric; it simply stopped him from withdrawal.

The drugs imbued the lyrics to his songs and parts of his art—images of poppies appeared in songs and paintings. And sometimes being high distorted his visions so much that his art was in disturbingly bad taste. One project was a huge canvas on to which he'd glued syringes. Kurt asked Rene Navarette what he thought of this particular work, and Navarette replied, "Well, if people see it, it's going to be pretty obvious." That creation, like many that Kurt started, was abandoned

ABOVE Kurt would occasionally dress in women's clothing and wear makeup. At this party, he is wearing one of Courtney's dresses. Dylan Carlson, Kurt's best friend, is standing above Kurt, and Mark Lanegan, singer for the Screaming Trees, is sitting below.

RIGHT Kurt was fascinated by drawing figures. He bought dozens, and he frequently cutomized them, as was the case with this example, onto which he has painted and etched lines with a knife.

FOLLOWING On this decorative, commercially printed landscape, Kurt wrote a line that would later end up in his song, "Frances Farmer Will Have Her Revenge On Seattle."

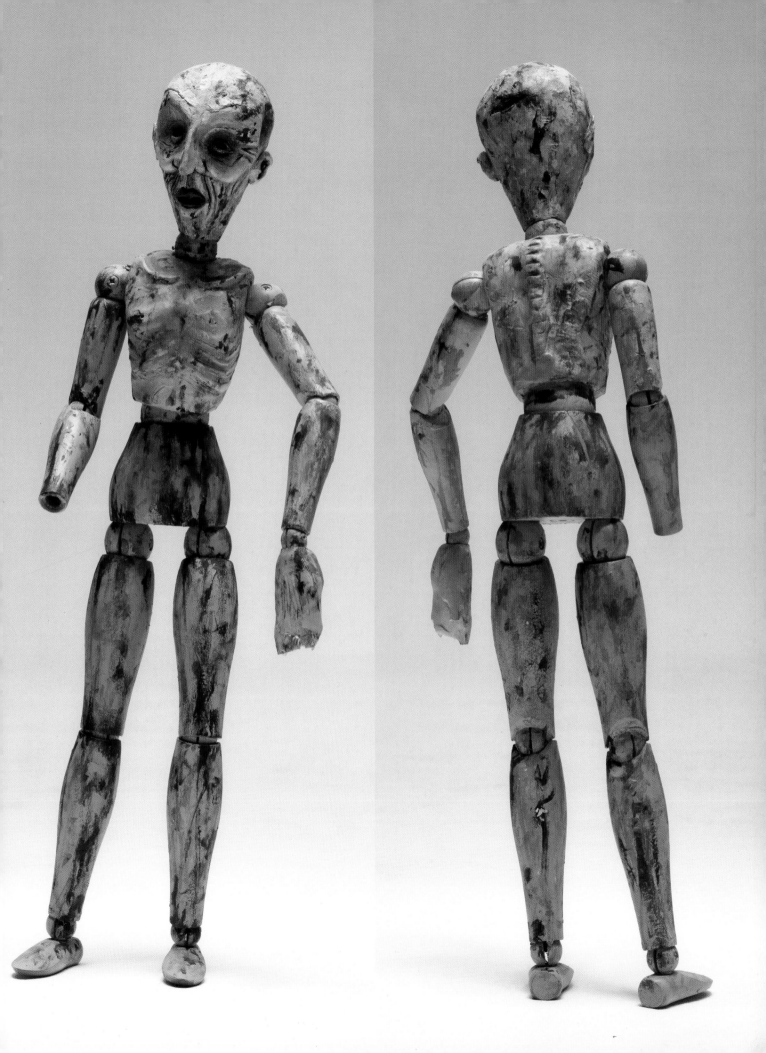

Frances Farmer will come ba

Fire to burn all the liars and leave a blanket of ash on the ground

Compact Disc Maxi-Single   Includes Complete Lyrics To Every Song On NEVERMIND

and later destroyed. Kurt had great impetus to start projects, but seemed to lack the will to complete anything.

His melancholy depressive moods seemed to alternate with frantic highs when he'd talk about his impending fatherhood. Yet even in that hopefulness, there was desperation in how he talked about the future. In a telling moment, Kurt purchased a bootleg videotape through the mail of an on-camera gunshot suicide. He watched this tape obsessively and snickered at the grisly death scene. He also used retail therapy to distract himself, going out one day and spending $10,000 on the latest video gear.

Money, which had been tight all of Kurt's life, had begun to roll in. *Nevermind* had taken on a life of its own and kept selling even without any promotional effort from the band. Though the album would always be listed in the 1991 music timelines, 1992 was its biggest commercial year. *Nevermind* had only sold about half a million copies when 1991 ended, but in the ensuing year it would rack up sales of another six million.

The money did have some benefits for Kurt's creativity. In addition to his painting supplies, he began to acquire expensive collectibles. He had always been a thrift store buyer, but now he had funds to peruse real antique stores or specialty shops. Anatomical figures had always been an obsession, but with funds to spare, Kurt began to buy life-sized professional quality body figures from medical supply centers. He also bought miniature plastic models of illustrated men and women, books on anatomy, and a life-sized CPR dummy and skeletons. His favorite anatomical collectibles were wooden figure-drawing models, and he bought dozens of these. He was obsessed with their alienlike visages, and their images, sometimes with faces added, often showed up in his paintings.

He also used his newfound wealth to enhance his album collection, which now stretched for many feet. He cherished punk albums by heroes like Black Flag or contemporaries like the Butthole Surfers, but he also bought children's and novelty records, like old U.S. Army commercial albums. At the same time, he began to buy oversized art books and had a particular fondness for tomes that collected the photographs of Diane Arbus. Rather than keep these expensive books in mint condition, Kurt would add words or slogans to the reproductions. To an Arbus photo of an overweight teen, he added the line "Riot Grrl" in large letters.

Doctoring his collectibles was as much fun as buying them. Kurt personalized many of the items to make them fit better into his traveling sideshow. On an album cover for pop crooner Debby Boone, he added a black mustache. On a transparent model of a human head, he painted the red markings of a superhero. On a wooden figure marionette, he painted facial features. Courtney also collected dolls, and he frequently took items from her stash and doctored these as well. He had always painted faces on his dolls, but in Los Angeles, he began to glue individual strands of his own hair to the figures' heads. Gluing other objects onto his creations—be it on an art canvas or a doll head—became one of his great passions. A few dolls even had animal teeth attached to the sides of their cheeks. His glue gun became as important to his art as his paintbrush.

He frequented hobby stores looking for the latest plastic model kits. Rather than cars or airplanes, he favored one-off sets that, when put into the context of his other oddities, would have an added meaning. For example, at a store that sold backdrops for trains or military dioramas, Kurt passed by the soldiers and purchased a plastic "Burned House" model that looked like something out of a miniature Hitchcock film set. Placed on his fireplace mantel next to an "Illustrated Woman" model, it had a particularly ghoulish effect.

Courtney's pregnancy unleashed a torrent of ideas and an avalanche of creativity in Kurt. He wasn't the first expectant parent to relish feeling more alive having created a life. Yet for Kurt, the idea of fatherhood was also filled with trepidation: He was worried about whether they'd have a "flipper baby," and he drew many drawings of mutated fetuses. This became such a fixation that Courtney eventually had to insist that he stop drawing the fetuses in front of her.

When Courtney had a sonogram, Kurt asked for both a print photograph and a video. He watched the video sonogram for hours, and Xeroxed the picture, painting around it as if to create a shrinelike offering to his unborn child. He nicknamed the child "Bean" because of the shape of the fetus. He later used the sonogram image on the sleeve for the "Lithium" CD single, which also featured one of Kurt's alien paintings on the cover. Reproduction had always been a theme in his

ABOVE Everything about the "Burned House" model from the name to the "hand weathered" notation appealed to Kurt's artistic sense of weird kitsch. It was one of the few models he left unopened and sealed—it was perfect as it was and required no Cobain-style alteration.

ENCLOSURE Kurt's collection included many masks. On this clear, full-sized face mask, he has painted and etched marks to resemble a Mexican wrestling mask.

OPPOSITE The majority of Kurt's models were of human body parts, like this anatomically correct "Human Heart." Eventually, Kurt began to order these models from distributors who supplied medical schools.

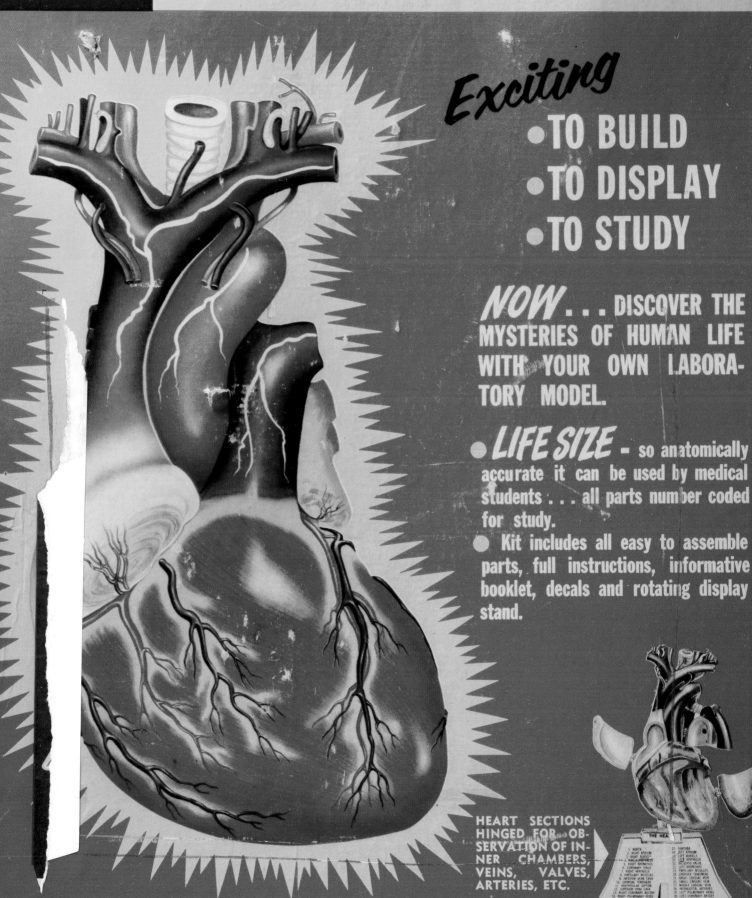

ABOVE In the fall of 1991, Kurt agreed to pose for the cover of *Rolling Stone*. By the time the photograph was to be shot, in February 1992 with Mark Seliger in Australia, Kurt had second thoughts. In an attempt to derail the session, he came wearing several humorous T-shirts, including this one, which reads "Kill the Grateful Dead." Kurt often repeated the line, "Bring me the blood of Jerry Garcia," in his diaries. Ironically, *Rolling Stone* found that another shot, where Kurt wore a T-shirt that read, "Corporate Magazines Still Suck," was more to their liking than this image, which was never published.

writing and art, but the pregnancy served to accelerate this obsession to the detriment of everything else, including, of course, Nirvana.

But Kurt's disinterest in Nirvana didn't stop the business entity of the band from progressing. Nirvana appeared on the cover of *Rolling Stone* in April, sourced from an interview done that winter. A new video was launched, and the band was nominated for numerous awards. Hardly a week went by when there wasn't a story published about the band, though Kurt rarely participated. Nirvana kept getting huge offers to go back on the road; Kurt turned them all down. One deal would have paid them over a million dollars for a few dates.

Kurt's decision not to tour alarmed his label and management. The *Los Angeles Times* ran an article on May 17, titled, "Why is Nirvana missing from a heavenly tour season?" Kurt frequently wouldn't answer the phone at his apartment, and if anyone wanted him for business purposes, they were forced to stop by. He often failed to answer the door, except for when heroin dealers came by at any hour. The dealers had an uncanny ability to show up during the periods Kurt was trying to kick drugs.

By March, Kurt was back in rehab at Cedars-Sinai. He was prescribed methadone to beat his cravings, but this effort, like many others, only helped temporarily. His drug counselors had recommended he try 12-Step meetings, but the idea of sitting in a room with strangers talking about his problems sounded worse to Kurt than the cost of the addiction. "That part of his personality probably got in the way of the recovery process," observed counselor Bob Timmons.

Between February and June, Nirvana virtually didn't exist, except through the commercial juggernaut that was the *Nevermind* album and a one-day recording session in Seattle where they cut two cover songs for compilations. Though Novoselic and Grohl were frustrated that the band wasn't touring, even they needed a break from the madness of the previous six months. Grohl told *Spin*, "Everything happened so fast. I don't think anyone knows what is going to happen next."

The fragile structure of the band suffered an even greater blow when Kurt decided they needed to readjust the percentages of royalties they each received from their songs—he asked for a larger share and threatened to quit if he didn't get his way. Novoselic and Grohl reluctantly agreed, though this one action forever changed the dynamic in what was once a band of brothers.

Pressure had built for Nirvana to tour, and eventually even Kurt felt he needed to act or risk losing their fan base. He put down the paintbrush and headed to Europe for several festival dates in June. He was on methadone again, but, despite his physical struggles, the band came back together easily and their shows were positively received. At the Reading Festival on August 30, Kurt rolled onstage in a wheelchair, his own little joke against all the naysayers who had reported him dead or too drug-sick to perform.

NIRVANA
RETURN OF THE RAT
RECORDED AT LAUNDRY ROOM STUDIOS
ENGINEERED BY BARRETT JONES
FROM THE WIPERS ALBUM: IS THIS REAL?
NIRVANA APPEARS COURTESY OF DGC RECORDS

NAPALM BEACH
POTENTIAL SUICIDE
M-99
ASTRO CLOUD
NIRVANA
RETURN OF THE RAT
POISON IDEA
UP FRONT
DHARMA BUMS
ON THE RUN
CRACKERBASH
I DON'T KNOW WHAT I AM / MYSTERY
HOLE
OVER THE EDGE
WHIRLEES
LAND OF THE LOST

T&K
RECORDS
TK 917010 TRIB 2
PO BOX 42423 • PORTLAND OR • 97242
NIRVANA AND HOLE APPEAR COURTESY OF D.G.C. RECORDS

ABOVE Much to the consternation of Nirvana's label, Kurt wasn't interested in recording another album in 1992, but that didn't stop the band from contributing to a box-set of singles put out by tiny indie label TK Records in Portland. The set benefited Greg Sage of the Wipers, an early Northwest punk pioneer Kurt admired.

WHILE THE BAND WAS IN EUROPE, Kurt and Courtney's Spaulding apartment flooded. A pipe in the apartment above them had burst and leaked into their unit. This was particularly painful to Kurt, who stored many of his paintings and paper artworks in their bathtub, thinking it a safe spot. He lost several journals and many sketches and pieces of art. The song lyrics were easier to reproduce than the art, much of which was destroyed for good.

They moved into another Los Angeles house, this one a rental on Alta Loma, in the Hollywood Hills. Unlike the Spaulding apartment, this home was more typical of what one might expect for a rock star—it was on a cliff and had been used as the location for Robert Altman's noirish film *The Long Goodbye*. Once again, Kurt set up a studio in the new home and, having more room, undertook larger paintings. "One of them was five feet by five feet," recalled Rene Navarette. "He was interested in bird images at the time; he was creating these great winged creatures."

They were living in the Alta Loma house on August 18, 1992, when Frances Bean was born. In interviews, Kurt cited his daughter as the thing in the world that gave him the most happiness and for which he felt the greatest pride. He said that often enough, to both reporters and friends, that he surely meant it. However, the circumstances of Frances's birth could not have been more strained. As Courtney's due date neared, the press hovered. Courtney made what she later called the biggest mistake of her life and allowed herself to be profiled in *Vanity Fair* magazine. That article suggested drug problems, and a Los Angeles County social worker was able to use this one magazine story as evidence to file a complaint against the couple.

Kurt, at least, *was* still struggling with drugs and, in what seemed like an almost comic twist, he was detoxing in the same hospital where Courtney was giving birth. She literally dragged him from his room, hauling him and his IV to the delivery center for the birth. It was less comical the next day, however, when he escaped the hospital detox, went out, bought drugs, and returned with a pistol. He was so afraid that their child would be taken from them, he attempted to convince Courtney to join him in a suicide pact. She grabbed the gun, and he fell weeping to the floor.

Frances was temporarily taken out of their legal custody, though that simply meant a relative had to be present in their house. Still, the experience forever changed the way Kurt and Courtney saw their relationship with the press, with management, and with the outside world. They had been publicly shamed, judged by the state to be unfit parents. No single event in Kurt's entire life caused him more anger. Though he'd written so many powerful songs about anger, he had rarely displayed much of it. With this betrayal, that shifted, and a fury arose in him that fueled both his art and music.

SOMETIME LATER IN 1992, Kurt sat down with his notebook and wrote out a cartoon that told the wild story of what had happened to his life that year. He drew two tiny caricatures of Courtney and

ABOVE Kurt, Courtney, and their new daughter, Frances, appeared on the cover of *Spin*, with Nirvana being named "Artist of the Year" for 1992, a year the band didn't release a studio album.

RIGHT Counterclockwise from top: Kurt and baby Frances in two snapshots taken by Courtney; Kurt insisted Frances be included in this news agency photo (he wrote "Diet Grrrl" on her stomach in washable marker, which was both a title he was considering for a song and a play on the Olympia "Riot Grrrl" movement).

himself. In the first panel, Kurt says to Courtney, "Will you help me tune my guitar? You're faster." "No problem," she replies. In the next panel, they kiss, and she says, "I love you, you're an asshole." He replies, "I love you, you're a bitch." The next panel shows platinum records on the wall and the narration: "Then came the money, the fame, the drugs, the scandal." Then a guy comes up to Kurt and asks, "Hey, aren't you Kurt Cobain?" "No man, I'm his twin," the cartoon man replies.

In the next panel, the two characters are in bed with syringes pointing at them and a bubble that reads, "We were happy on drugs, but had to stop. It just got too sick. So we had a little girl baby." The final panel is a reference to the magazine story that would haunt Kurt for all of his days: "And got a lot of shit." Kurt's little caricature is reading a magazine titled, *Vanity-is-not-fair-to-anyone, humility is.*

Many of the songs Kurt wrote that year reflect his increasingly cynical worldview. In "All Apologies," for example, Kurt sarcastically wrote that he would take the blame for every ill of the world—it was as if he were crucifying himself. "Serve the Servants," even more to the point, spews, "Self appointed judges judge more than they have sold." "Rape Me," though initially written before *Nevermind*'s release, was revised; the added lyrics seemed timely considering the *Vanity Fair* violation, as they referenced "my favorite inside source," a dart thrown at those who talked anonymously to the press but declined to confront the couple directly. "Rape Me" became the centerpiece of the group's shows. "Hate me," Kurt sang, "do it and do it again." The song had begun as Kurt's attempt to describe the subjugation of women in society, but he sang it as if he were the one violated.

After Frances's birth, Kurt entered rehab for a third time. The treatment program allowed him to leave for Nirvana business and to see Frances and Courtney. An appearance in September at the MTV Video Music Awards was triumphant, despite some backstage drama that included a run-in with Axl Rose.

A week after the MTV Awards, Kurt did an interview with Robert Hilburn of the *Los Angeles Times,* during which he talked about his drug struggles with the press for the first time. He said he "chose to use drugs," and he urged kids never to get caught up in them. He downplayed the extent of his addiction, but in moving toward accountability, his actions indicated that his treatment was beginning to work. He said the band's next album would be "really raw," and that he didn't think he'd do long tours again. "I would rather be healthy and alive," he said. "I don't want to sacrifice myself or my family."

Mostly, he talked about Frances and what a joy she had been to him. "I knew that when I had a child, I'd be overwhelmed, and it's true. . . . I can't tell you how much my attitude has changed since we've got Frances." He ended the interview with the one line that would appear in all the hundreds of other newspapers and magazines that reprinted or referenced the interview: "Holding my baby is the best drug in the world." ■

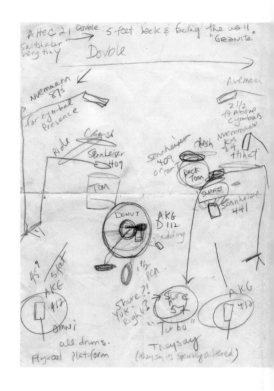

TOP LEFT Kurt, Frances, and Hole drummer Patty Schemel, who grew close to the family after living with them during much of the year after Frances's birth.

BOTTOM LEFT Frances with Kurt and his ever-present Sonic Youth T-shirt.

ABOVE Kurt methodically drew recommendations for Patty Schemel on how he thought the drums should be recorded for Hole's *Live Through This.*

FOLLOWING Kurt and Frances Bean, 1992.

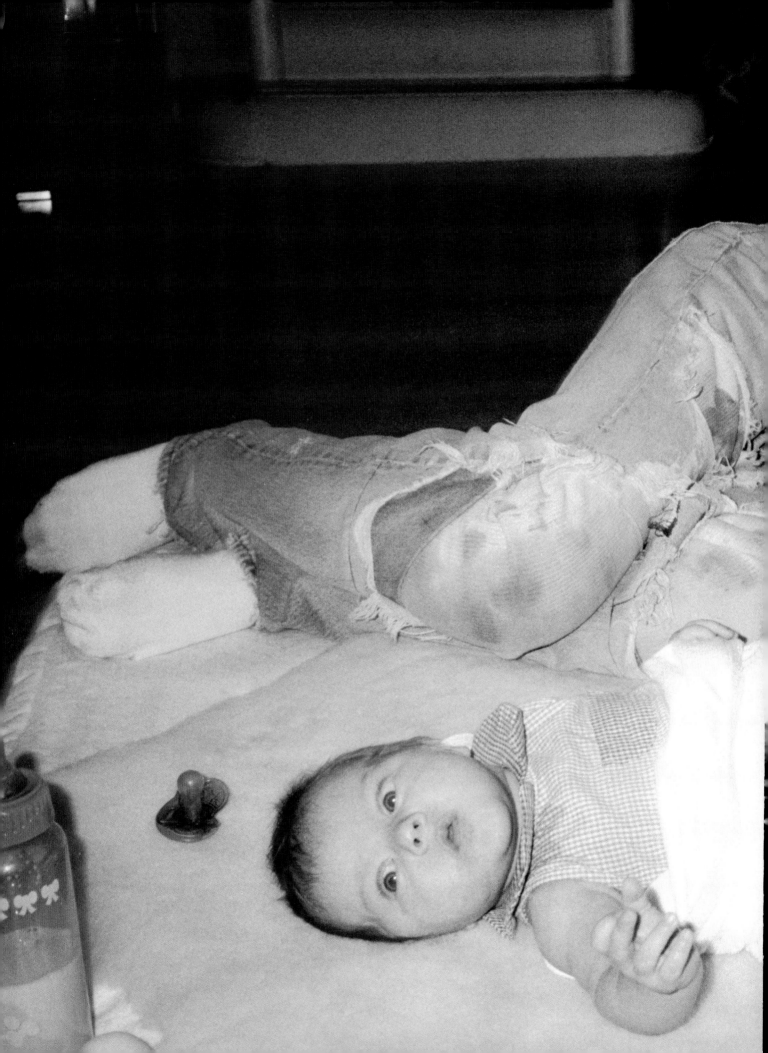

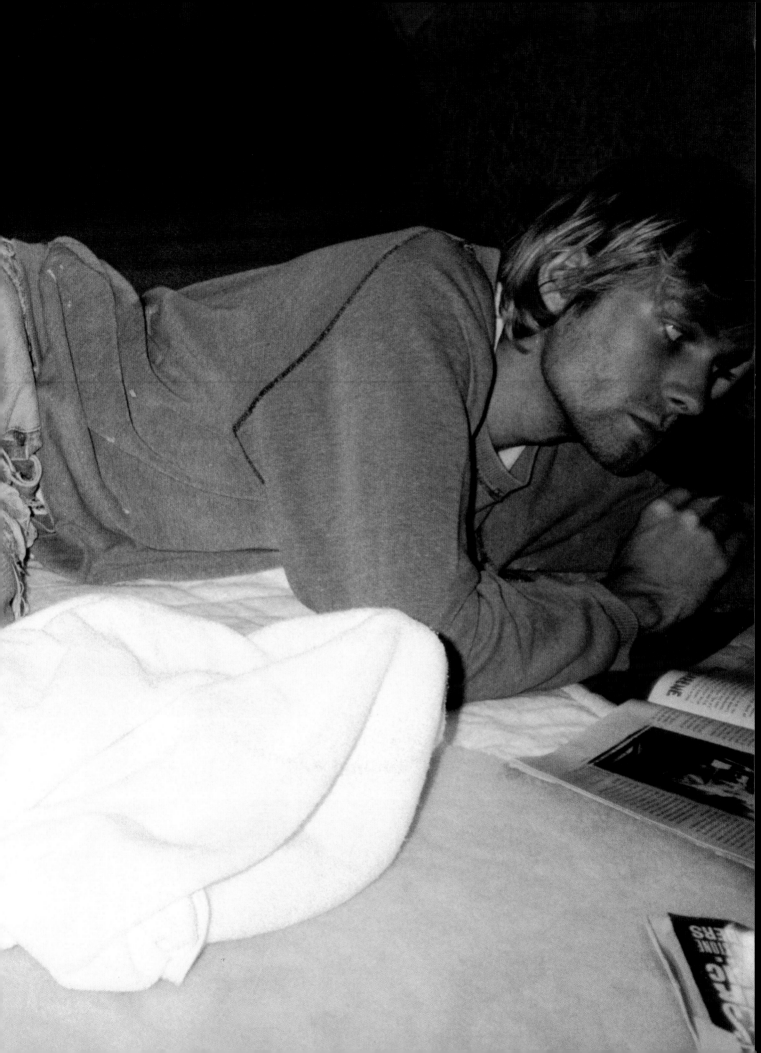

9

ENGAGINGLY LOST

I n his home in the Hollywood Hills in the fall of 1992, Kurt began to create something that didn't come to him as easily as the music and art projects he'd conjured up all his life: He was now making a family. Like many children of divorce, he took fatherhood and marriage extremely seriously and pledged that he would do better than his own parents had. Initially, that meant learning how to change diapers, plus making sure that Frances had the ideal toys, car seats, and onesies. And though Kurt did change diapers, the Cobains also hired a twenty-four-hour-a-day nanny who helped when the strains of parenthood and rock stardom collided.

Being a parent changed Kurt's own self-image and his internal dialogue. He had always been filled with self-doubt, which increased with the birth of his daughter, as he pondered whether he was a fit parent. Occasionally, however, fatherhood had a positive effect, helping to abate his fears and giving him a rare optimism about the world. While he had always been empathetic in his love for animals, he hadn't had much experience with children, other than a brief stint working for the Aberdeen YMCA. He was proud of Frances Bean, and equally proud, at times, that he was capable of such nurturing. "I'll go out of my way to remind her that I love her more than I love myself," he wrote in his journal. "Not because it's a father's duty, but because I want to out of love." The very language of that entry showed a change in the way Kurt talked to himself and a directness that had been missing before the birth of his daughter.

In a later interview with *Kerrang,* Kurt addressed the effect Frances had on his moods. "I've always been chronically depressed, or at least pessimistic, for a part of each day," he said. "Now I only have to see Frances for ten minutes, and my spirits are lifted so high I feel like a different person." Though his depression did not lift for long, his daughter gave his life a much-needed jolt of meaning, the absence of which he had often felt since his own childhood.

Other than in his overflowing journals, Kurt had not often chronicled his own life with personal photographs, but with Frances's birth, he began to write less in his journal and, instead, to photograph and film his family. He took snapshots, Polaroids, and videos of the baby's first bath,

RIGHT Kurt took this photograph of his sneakers and Frances in a playpen at the end of his bed. He had applied gel to his daughter's hair. The image on the wall is a poster issued by a gun shop for target practice; Kurt added a subtle "K Records" logo on the man's lapel.

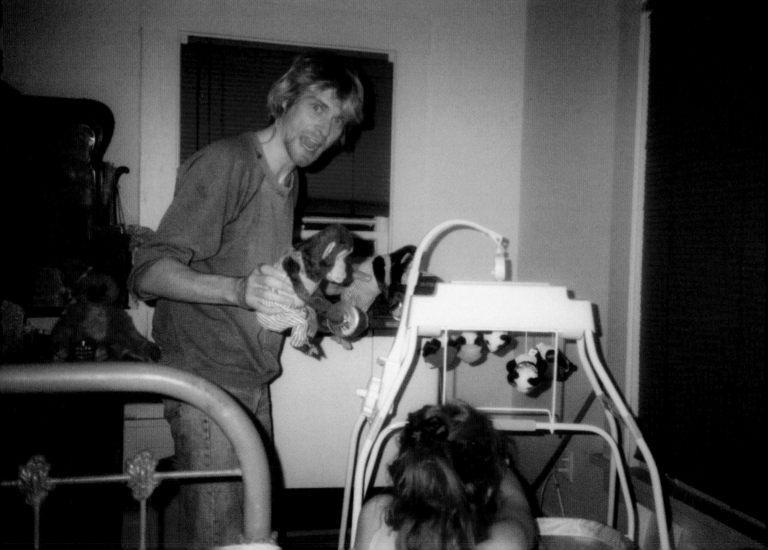

OUTSIDE FLAP An early running order for *In Utero*, which Kurt was then calling *I Hate Myself and I Want to Die*. Several of the songs on the album went through name changes, including "Heart-Shaped Box," which Kurt initially called "Heart-Shaped Coffin." Kurt had a song titled "Formula," and he considered that title, and the line "twenty-four notes, six strings, and thirty years," as potential album names prior to settling on *In Utero*.

INSIDE FLAP AND RIGHT A small sampling of Kurt's personal collection of cassette tapes. He often recorded demos of songs over tapes of other bands, and he frequently decorated his cassette covers. Included in this pile are very early tapes, such as the "Fecal Matter" original demo and acoustic demos recorded in 1993.

CD Along with music, Kurt recorded hundreds of hours of spoken-word monologues, sometimes including sound effects or music riffs, but other times simply using his voice. At least twice he was broadcast on the Olympia radio station KAOS, doing his spoken-word performance. He titled one of these experiments "Montage of Heck," yet another one of the many names he had considered for his band. The enclosed eight-minute sampling on this CD single is one of the more straightforward of Kurt's spoken-word recordings, in which he narrates one of his cartoons, "Crybaby Jerkins," and laughs as he reads excerpts from his journals. The CD sleeve shows the "Crybaby Jerkins" cartoon. The second track on the CD is an interview between author Charles R. Cross and KUOW radio's Marcie Sillman on Kurt Cobain's journals, recordings, and the making of this book.

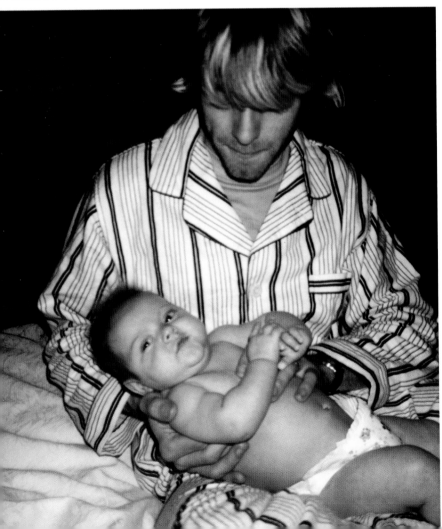

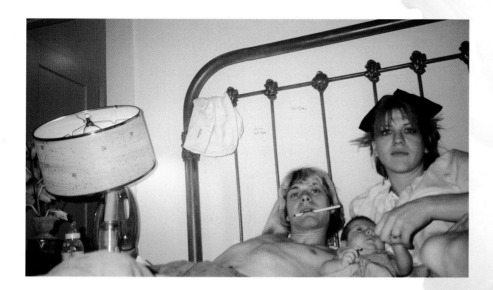

conception of the album was the opposite of how he had approached what he was now calling the "candy-assed" pop of *Nevermind*. Whereas he had wanted the world to come to *Nevermind*, he now wanted to scare away his former audience with the sound of the next record. He wanted to title the new album *I Hate Myself and I Want to Die,* and he initially conceived of it as Nirvana's return to punk. Early in preproduction, he sat down and wrote a list of some of the songs he was considering, and their names alone were designed to shock: "Heart-Shaped Coffin," "Nine Month Media Blackout," "Macro Antibiotic," "Dumb," and "Moist Vagina." To the latter song title he added the notation, "then she blew him like he's never been blown, brains stuck all over the wall."

Much of the lyric writing, however, was laser-sharp, with the final results reflecting fully realized songs that had depth. "Pennyroyal Tea" was a traditionally composed ballad, another anti-love love song, but this time around it was about an abortion-inducing herb. With lyrics like "I have very bad posture," Kurt managed to make the song both personal and universal. The lyrics and melody were so catchy that a listener might be caught off guard by the song's topic. He'd written catchy songs before about torture and rape—now he added abortion to that oeuvre.

"Heart-Shaped Coffin" evolved into "Heart-Shaped Box," a reference to the mementos that Kurt and Courtney collected. She had given him a heart-shaped box on one of their first dates, so the title for them had romantic significance. Musically, Kurt had finally come up with a melody that would have fit in the Lennon/McCartney songbook. Married with lyrics like "I wish I could eat your cancer," the result was catchy, disturbing, and unique. "Heart-Shaped Box" might be the best example of Kurt's gift of creating pop music with a dark twist—the same fucked-up twist that was in his art—and was the apogee of the new album. Kurt was obsessed with the idea of rock's formula; he'd even wanted to use the title "Formula" for "Drain You." Yet despite his frequent criticism that

TOP LEFT Kurt serenades Frances, Los Angeles, 1992.

BOTTOM LEFT AND FAR LEFT The Cobains spent several months in the winter of 1993 living in various Seattle five-star hotels, including the Four Seasons Olympic.

ABOVE Kurt, Frances, and Courtney in their home in Los Angeles, late 1992. Written on the wall behind the bed is a message for Courtney to call a journalist for a scheduled interview.

VIP

ROMANTIC POSE

AFTER SHOW

by lady
stick

NIRVANA

REPRODUCTION

rock was dead, he managed to take the same "twenty-four notes, six strings, and thirty years" he thought had strangled the form and to make something new and vibrant with them.

The songwriting, however, was less controversial than how Kurt wanted the album recorded: He insisted that it be cut in a lo-fi manner, which he felt would alienate all but his truest fans. In his journal, he wrote out a marketing plan that would have the album released initially on vinyl, cassette, and eight-track tape only. After what he expected to be "lame reviews," he then planned to release a remixed version that sounded better on compact disc.

Though early demos for the album were done with producer Jack Endino in Seattle, there was only one producer who was obnoxious enough to make the entire album Kurt wanted, and that was Steve Albini. Albini didn't even call himself a producer and insisted his credit be "Recorded by." Albini's current band was called Rapeman; as a teenager, Kurt had seen the last show ever done by Albini's earlier group, Big Black.

In 1992, Kurt often stated in interviews that Albini would be the producer of the next Nirvana album, but Kurt hadn't bothered to actually contact Albini to see if he'd agree. Albini had a curmudgeonly personality similar to Cobain's, and he got angry seeing his name bandied around. Albini issued a press release insisting that he was in fact *not* recording the next Nirvana album. Almost as soon as Albini issued his release, DGC contacted him and offered him a $100,000 fee, which he accepted. Having two competing press releases in one week—one where Albini disowned the project and another that announced his hiring—was only the first of many controversies that would evolve around the album.

Albini's condition for doing the album was that the band would agree to be isolated in a rural studio away from their friends, families, and, in Kurt's case, drug dealers. The band agreed and, in February 1993, headed to Pachyderm Studio in Cannon Falls, Minnesota, forty miles outside of

LEFT Kurt's newfound wealth and fame did little to change the way he dressed. Here he is wearing a T-shirt that he was given for free from the U.K. music magazine *Sounds*.

ABOVE By early 1992 the band was beginning to fracture, and though they still posed for group photos, it was rare to see the three band members hanging out. Even their group photos displayed tension.

ENCLOSURE A backstage pass. Kurt infrequently appeared at backstage meet-and-greets.

art in that it was thematically disturbing, displayed stylistic talent, and was evocative of multiple interpretations, the most obvious being that it centered on addiction.

In March of 1993, the family moved to a rental house in the Lake City neighborhood of Seattle, marking the first time that Kurt officially had a Seattle address. It was a 6,000-square-foot home with enough space for their various nannies and for Kurt to spread out his things. One room became Kurt's project space, immediately scattered with painting supplies and various collectibles. Kurt was still obsessed with the idea of creating his own fanzine and continued to clip things from other publications that he thought he might use as part of a collage in his. Despite the frequent talk, he never managed to create his own publication.

While in the Lake City house, the Cobains' long battle with the state of California finally came to an end: On March 25, 1993, the state dropped its monitoring of Frances. When Courtney added up the total costs of the case—all stemming from one article in *Vanity Fair*—they had spent over $240,000 on legal bills alone. Nirvana also had to suffer the indignity of being sued that year by an obscure sixties band who had used the name Nirvana two decades before. The case was settled, but the cost to Kurt and his bandmates was well over $100,000.

Kurt spent most of that spring working on projects involving *In Utero*. He was insistent that he create the album cover this time around, and the label gave in. He met with the label's art department and brought a postcard of one of the many illustrated models he collected, a

FLAP Kurt worked harder on the back cover art for *In Utero* than he had on any single other visual artistic effort in his life, spending days trying to get the positioning of all the elements exact. He methodically assembled his doll collection, flowers, and the turtle shell. Once he felt it was ready, he called up Charles Peterson and insisted the photographer come shoot the image that day, before the flowers wilted. One of the biggest problems during the shoot was keeping Frances from playing with the installation.

ABOVE Kurt took these Polaroids of his installation.

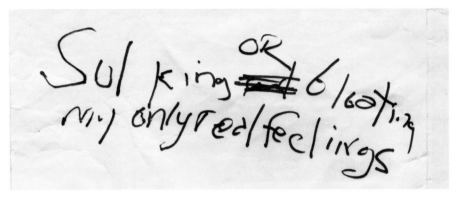

transparent anatomical female manikin. Rights to the image were obtained, and a freelance artist later added wings to the female figure. Ironically, the winged woman bears resemblance to a photograph Kurt had taken of a naked Courtney around that time, when he posed her with a light under a towel, creating a winglike effect. He often photographed his wife nude, before and after sex, perhaps finding the visual capture of her another part of their eroticism.

For the back cover, Kurt assembled a collage of his many plastic dolls in his garage over the course of several weeks. He called the work, "Sex and woman and *In Utero* and vaginas and birth and death." In a way, the title aptly summed up his entire oeuvre. The work was roughly four feet by six feet, one of the larger pieces Kurt had ever created. His initial design idea was to use Popsicle sticks to connect the foldout panels in the CD booklet. Kurt's final touch was $200 worth of flowers, which he added to the piece before it was photographed. Charles Peterson shot the image, and the label later changed the color to an orange tint. Kurt, Courtney, and Frances all watched the photography session, and some photos from that day show the family toying with the doll creations. Many of the items weren't glued down and the art shifted as Frances played with them. She grew up as accustomed to fetus models as most little girls were to Barbie dolls.

In conceiving of the album, Kurt had also planned an image for the first single, slated to be "Heart-Shaped Box." He brought the label a photo that he'd processed at a one-hour lab, which showed a heart-shaped box on top of aluminum foil and flowers. By that point, he and Courtney owned over two dozen different variations of heart-shaped boxes—it was one of the few collectible items they agreed upon. "There was always a strange contrast in what they collected," observed Patty Schemel. "You had this Laura Ashley, girlie stuff that Courtney liked, and next to it there would be a Colonel Sanders figurine that Kurt had collected. A lot of his stuff had a kitschy feel, with a strong sense of humor to them." Not everything that Kurt created or said was done with complete seriousness, and those who knew him closely described him as wickedly funny in a sarcastic way. Irony was a big part of his humor and his worldview. "Make a joke out of irony, and a fool out of God," he wrote in one journal entry.

ABOVE LEFT A small scrap from Kurt's diary.

ABOVE AND RIGHT Both Kurt and Courtney collected heart-shaped boxes, and by 1994 they had several dozen in their home. They often gave them to each other as gifts, sometimes filled with personal effects such as hair or a note, or on other occasions containing antique valentines. The white silk box (above) was the first gift Courtney ever gave to Kurt.

The Priest
they called
him

William S Burroughs   1972

 irvana's new album was released in September of 1993 to almost universally rave reviews. "Brilliant, corrosive, enraged, and thoughtful, most of them all at once," *Rolling Stone* said of *In Utero*. "More than anything else, it's a triumph of the will." Despite Kurt's plan to create a record that would alienate his fans, it entered the *Billboard* charts at Number 1 and sold 180,000 copies in the first week alone.

That number was impressive, particularly considering that two of the biggest record chains did not initially stock the album. Wal-Mart and Kmart had objected to Kurt's back-cover art, finding his image of fetuses and dolls too offensive. Both chains had also asked that some of the song titles be changed, specifically "Rape Me." Kurt's management called him and suggested that they produce a watered-down version of the cover: The music would be the same, but they'd edit Kurt's back-cover art to remove the fetuses and change the title of "Rape Me" to "Waif Me."

To suggest this kind of artistic compromise to an iconoclast like Kurt Cobain must have taken an incredible amount of nerve—comanager Danny Goldberg reported that he made the call. But even more shocking was Kurt's reply: "When I was a kid, I could only go to Wal-Mart," Kurt told Goldberg. "I want the kids to be able to get this record. I'll do what they want." Kurt's explanation, whatever its motivation, wasn't true: The Aberdeen Wal-Mart opened long after Kurt moved away.

Perhaps more important, Kurt's quick compromise showed a shift. Wracked by fear of scarcity, legal woes, and conflict, Kurt was no longer as sure of himself as he'd been back in his Olympia apartment when he was first plotting his career. His controversial art and music had also been a source of problems for him, even as it had brought him wealth and fame. Perhaps most disturbing to him that season was a lawsuit over the "Heart-Shaped Box" video. The original director had been replaced and had filed a copyright infringement suit, arguing that ideas from an early treatment were used in the final video. Kurt was terrified that this suit would bankrupt him, and he repeatedly mentioned this fear to those close to him.

RIGHT When it came time to promote *In Utero*, Kurt only agreed to do a handful of photo sessions. Most were with fashion photographers, who often brought elaborate props, including, in this instance, a tiger suit. Kurt's nail polish had started to chip.

ABOVE Fall 1992, at a photo session for *Monk* magazine. The magazine's editors had brought a logger outfit, complete with a chainsaw, which Kurt agreed to pose with. At one point during the shoot, Kurt said he wanted a latte and went to a stand near the photo studio. When he got there, he offered to serve as barista. "He made us all a cup of coffee," recalled photographer Charlie Hoselton.

There were, of course, real specters that haunted him in the form of his addiction. There were several overdoses that year, including one on May 9, 1993, that was severe enough that paramedics were called and Kurt was taken to the hospital. Even some of Kurt's drug buddies became alarmed at how much heroin he was using. "He definitely used a lot of dope," observed Dylan Carlson, Kurt's best friend. In another drug-fueled fiasco, Kurt was arrested for domestic violence that summer. He was still the biggest rock star in the world, in the middle of doing advance press for *In Utero*, but his life was falling apart.

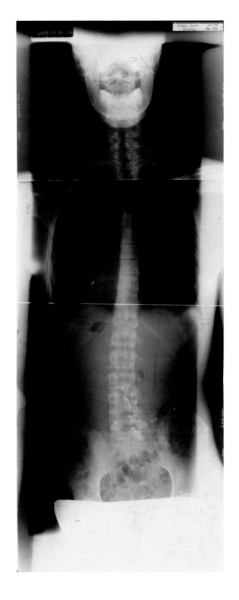

When he was a teenager, Kurt held the belief that drugs helped fuel creativity, but by 1991, he had grown to question that conviction. As his addiction became debilitating, it took him away from his family, his band, and his art. By the fall of 1993, he attempted few creative projects, only composed a handful of songs, and rarely wrote in his journal. Of the few journal entries he penned, many were about how hard it was to quit drugs and what a hell they had caused his life to be. "The psychological factors have set in and are as damaging as the physical effects," he wrote in one treatise. "Every time you kick, as time goes by, it gets more uncomfortable. Even the most needle-phobic person can crave the relief of putting a syringe in their arm."

Kurt was still seeking help from addiction doctors, but he never stuck with any treatment plan for more than a few days. He was also continually haunted by his other medical woes: stomach, depression, back pain. The "I have very bad posture" lyric from "Pennyroyal Tea" was no joke; Kurt's back problems, first identified in his childhood, caused him to ache many days. He had X-rays taken in September 1993, and they showed that his spine still had a curvature indicative of scoliosis. In his journals, he reflected back on his teenaged years often and frequently addressed his aches. "My bones were growing and it hurt really bad," he wrote in one passage. His pains—some structural and some caused by his growing addiction—were with him always.

THE LONGTIME THEORY OF MOST ROCK BANDS, dating back to the days of Buddy Holly, was that a band needed to tour to promote an album. Playing live was a major source of revenue for Nirvana, both from ticket sales and merchandising. Kurt's manager estimated that as much as a million dollars could be made from merchandising alone on a 1993 tour. A tour would help the sales of *In Utero* as well, which had stalled a bit after a fast start.

Kurt did not want to tour, and he said as much to his managers and bandmates. "He said he didn't want to go," his lawyer Rosemary Carroll recalled. "And frankly, he was pressured to go." That pressure came from his label, his bandmates, his wife, and the dozen people in the crew who counted on Nirvana for their living. No one knew whether it was better to force Kurt to go cold turkey on tour, or whether he should be allowed to stay home and sink deeper into his drug retreat.

ABOVE Kurt suffered from back problems throughout his life, and in May 1993, he sought out a specialist. This X-ray indicates his childhood scoliosis was still present and the curvature of his spine was no doubt furthered by years of playing a heavy guitar.

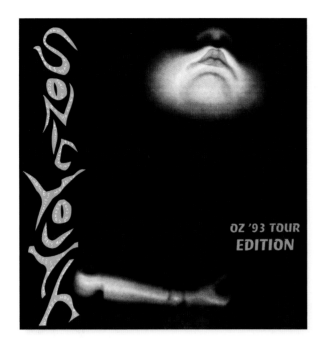

Finally, Kurt agreed to go on the road. Just prior to the tour, when MTV asked him why they were playing large arenas, he responded with an answer that said much about why he agreed to a tour he didn't want to do: "We're not nearly as rich as everyone thinks we are."

The band set off in September for a world tour that would include over seventy scheduled dates. Initially, Kurt's spirits improved, as creating the *In Utero* live show forced him to be artistic again. For the first time, Kurt designed an elaborate stage set, which included the life-sized anatomical figure from the album cover and spooky *Wizard of Oz*–type trees. A cello player was added to the band, and guitarist Pat Smear joined as a second guitar player. Those changes were designed to put less pressure on Kurt, and initially they seemed to work.

During the second week of the tour, after a show in Chicago, Kurt talked about his fragile health to *Rolling Stone*'s David Fricke. "My stomach ailment has been one of the biggest barriers that has stopped us from touring," he said. "After a person experiences chronic pain for five years, by the time that fifth year ends, you're literally insane. I couldn't cope with anything."

In the same interview, Kurt mentioned that the press generally wrote about him as if he were "a pissy, complaining, freaked-out schizophrenic who wants to kill himself all the time." Fricke asked if Kurt was truly suicidal. "For five years during the time I had my stomach problem, yeah," he said. "I wanted to kill myself every day. I came very close many times. I'm sorry to be so blunt about it. . . . This is no way to live a life. I love to play music, but something was not right. So I decided to medicate myself." Fricke noted that there were many kids in Nirvana's audience who also suffered from angst and suicidal thoughts. "That pretty much defines our band," Kurt continued. "It's both those contradictions. It's satirical and it's serious at the same time."

ABOVE Kurt contributed the cover art for this Sonic Youth EP that was initially only issued on vinyl in Australia. Though the EP had limited distribution, Kurt was extremely proud to have his art featured and to be formally connected to a band he worshipped.

RIGHT By late 1993, Kurt rarely ventured forth without Bono-type sunglasses. If his goal was to make himself more anonymous, the glasses had the opposite effect.

THE SECOND WEEK OF NOVEMBER, the band was in New York, and a review of their show in the *New York Times* illustrated the precarious position Kurt was in. It read, in part: "Mr. Cobain has presented himself as the reluctant pop performer (though a stage seems like an odd place to hide), and in performance he tries his best to come off like an anti-star, standing still for the most part, and drawling his words unemotionally. But there is no escape from the pop mechanism, and Mr. Cobain hasn't quite come to terms with it."

The *Times* review echoed a comment George Bernard Shaw once said of T. E. Lawrence, who became the legendary "Lawrence of Arabia" because of press coverage. When Lawrence was in the middle of the stage, Shaw suggested, "with ten limelights blazing on him, everyone pointed at him and said: 'See! He is hiding. He hates publicity.'" Kurt similarly wanted to be an "anti-star," in that he sought all the trappings of stardom—fame, money, and power—yet chose to give the impression that none of these things mattered to him. His use of the media, which was mostly complicit in his manipulation, was in a way as extraordinary as his musical accomplishments.

Press like the *Times* piece outraged Kurt, who read all of his reviews, and it may have been one reason he was so sour the next day when the band began rehearsals for the MTV show *Unplugged.* Kurt had only agreed to the program after much hounding, and he had asked that the Meat Puppets accompany Nirvana. He wanted to upend the Nirvana he had created and to present a stripped-down band as a way to defy expectations.

ABOVE Kurt, Courtney, and Frances were the most photographed celebrities at the 1993 MTV Video Music Awards. Even Ru Paul stopped by to pay homage.

RIGHT A diary entry from 1993.

for New Complaint songs :
record the quiet verses on a
boom box. Then ~~over~~ when
the loud parts come in record it on
~~a~~ normal studio tracks

use once And destroy

I'd like to have you murdered but Its illegal
and I'm too tired. and lazy

She eyes me like
A pisces
I cant stop the growth of her cancer

set out to green pastor   speaking in bitten tongue
A hole
kickin the teeth of a foot swallowed whole

like A Hairy man in A dress

Unplugged was one of the most somber Nirvana concerts ever, and it felt like an ending rather than a new beginning. Kurt had insisted the stage be decorated with black candles, chandeliers, and Stargazer lilies, which he said were his favorite flowers. "Like a funeral?" one producer had asked Kurt. "Exactly," he replied.

Despite Kurt's initial jitters, the performance was transcendent. In recreating his hits as acoustic ballads, he demonstrated that lyric storytelling was at the heart of many of his songs. And the last song of the night was rendered so slowly it *was* funereal. Kurt had chosen his cover of Leadbelly's "Where Did You Sleep Last Night," and he wrenched every bit of emotion from the dark lyrics. A few in the audience at the taping could be seen crying. In the seven years that had passed since Kurt's first public performance, he had learned how to read a crowd and how to use his music to leave them weeping.

The melancholy of the *Unplugged* set hid a personal struggle that those who watched the show in the studio, or later on when it was broadcast, didn't know about: The very day of the taping, Kurt's stomach problems had recurred—throughout his adult life they came and went

LEFT On December 13, 1993, Nirvana played a Seattle concert filmed for MTV's "Live and Loud" New Year's show. Alice Wheeler, who had been photographing Kurt since his very first photo session, shot this intimate portrait of Frances reaching for her father's sunglasses.

ABOVE Kurt with Nirvana roadie and former Exploited guitarist, "Big John" Duncan. Duncan played four songs with Nirvana at a 1993 New York concert, and the success of that experiment encouraged Kurt to hire Pat Smear of the Germs as a rhythm guitarist.

R.E.M./ATHENS, LTD.
ATHENS, GEORGIA 30603

Hey, Kurt

Heres a bunch of stuff we
talked about theres tee shirts
for all nirvanas & spouses & one
for cali

I found your ring (actually, Lynda
found it in the cabin) and I'm
giving it to David, my friend with
cancer, today. It will mean a lot, I'm
telling him the whole story.

I really dig finally getting to talk
to you & hope to keep in touch.

Love &
SHIT

Michael

LEFT Nirvana's legendary *Unplugged* concert in New York on November 18, 1993.

ABOVE A letter from R.E.M.'s Michael Stipe to Kurt, circa 1993. The two quickly became friends, and Stipe was one of Kurt's few friends who understood the pressures of fame. During early 1994, the two were planning a musical collaboration. Several dates were set for studio time, and although Stipe went as far as to send Kurt an airplane ticket, Kurt never made the trip, and the musical union never happened.

with a maddening irregularity. He was distraught, and once again he began the routine of seeing doctors and taking tests. Writing in his journal around that time, he said he'd give up on hit records if only his ailments could be diagnosed. "Just let me have my very own unexplainable rare stomach disease named after me."

The tour continued until a Christmas break, whereupon Kurt and Courtney escaped to the exclusive Canyon Ranch Spa for several days. Kurt attempted his own detox and saw an addiction specialist who quoted Shakespeare. Kurt was told he could either be or not be. In other words, he could either kick drugs for good or risk death from their continued ravages. ∎

Kurt began his New Year with some optimism, as in early January 1994, Kurt and Courtney bought their first home. It was an elegant fifteen-room mansion in the tony Denny-Blaine neighborhood near Lake Washington. At over 7,000 square feet, it was even larger than their previous rental, and Kurt's things were quickly spread out to fill the space, with art projects occupying many of the nooks and corners. They moved Kurt's drum set and a karaoke machine to the basement, and that was where Kurt often went to create.

The mansion, which had been built in 1902, was almost too large, however, and the Cobains' lack of furniture initially gave it a spooky and cavernous feel. To add to the eeriness, Kurt had recently purchased a life-sized wax replica of Lizzie Borden. He would stick the figure in a corner or have it stare out the window, telling Courtney that it would scare away intruders. The house was next to a public park, and though a hedge surrounded most of it, the one thing it lacked was privacy. Kurt said he was worried about burglars and used this as a justification for the several guns that he owned.

The Cobains had paid $1,130,000 for the home and had a mortgage of over a million dollars. This was a far cry from just a few years previous when Kurt could hardly scrape together $137 a month for the shoebox-sized Olympia apartment. Despite having over a million dollars now in his Charles Schwab brokerage account, Kurt was still worried that the lawsuit over the "Heart-Shaped Box" video would bankrupt him, forcing him to give up the house he had just bought.

At their new address, Kurt and Courtney continued their habit of writing on the walls, though they did attempt to keep a semblance of order to the home. Kurt had written a sheet of "laws of the estate" for their nannies, assistants, bandmates, and various others who seemed to come and go at all hours, and posted it on the wall. It was titled: "Rules. Mr. Tightwad sez: Disregard due to true un-importance." Among the rules was "No scribbling on the walls unless to measure height of frames." Kurt also implored all to have "more respect for cigarettes," fearful that someone would start a fire by

RIGHT Frances accompanied Kurt on some of the early dates of the *In Utero* tour, and her presence mellowed him considerably. During the concerts, Kurt insisted she wear oversized ear protectors.

Rules

→ KURT

Hey Courtney —

out of a whim I stopped here
hoping for some inspiration. Your door
is open but I couldn't wait for a response
once again Thankyou for everlasting
support. & inspiration — I may move here
soon in scope of music.
please call soon
♡ DD again
(sobaddicted)

Kisses etc
XXOOXOOO

Hey Jerry A called
we — ?!??!

MR Tightwad Disregard
Sez: Due to True
Unimportance

LAWS of the whm Estate, vital for it's profitable gain & growth.
in the vein of Jack Webb (Sgt Friday (Dragnet)) & a pinch of Archie Bunker

Here Are the Laymans terms:

DO Not let garbage get out of hand. help to bring firewood in to the house
dispose of excess garbage use this bulletin board as the tool for messages memos, reminders.
A trash can in every room to be used incessant
NO scribbling on walls unless to measure height of frames.
obsessively. More respect for cigarettes. make a conscious effort to keep track of checkbooks, keys, credit ca
Lock All doors at all times we will discuss a secret hiding place for spare keys. use alarm
Again always lock doors. become more of a tightwad for the betterment of the Family.
(the ashtrays not behind the couch.
Lets bring back innocence with the nihilism of today which is irony.
work on systems that will relieve petty, unnecessary waste and indulgence.

U.R. FINE!
Bb Daddy.

Messages:

A Garbage in every Room
to be used all the time!

leaving a lit butt on a floor—Courtney had burned down two of her previous residences back when she lived in Portland. A garbage can was considered necessary in every room, and ashtrays were to be used, "not behind the couch." Near the end, Kurt wrote a line that suggested his scarcity issues were still rampant in his new million-dollar mansion: "Become more of a tightwad for the betterment of the family. Let's bring back innocence with the nihilism of the day, which is irony. Work on systems that will relieve, petty, unnecessary waste and indulgence."

Kurt didn't have much time to enjoy the new home, because almost immediately after they moved in, the *In Utero* tour began anew in Europe. Kurt approached this leg of the tour with even more reluctance than the U.S. segment. Before touring began, he was already complaining of a sore throat.

THOUGH THE FIRST SHOW IN LISBON WENT WELL, after only the second concert, Kurt was visiting local physicians complaining of various ailments. His stomach was hurting, his throat was sore, and he desperately hoped to find a sympathetic doctor who might give him something to help with withdrawal. When visiting one physician failed to bring the desired result, he'd simply find another. In Europe, addiction is treated more as a disease than as a moral failing—as many in America choose to view it—so occasionally European doctors would give him sedatives. The drugs were no longer making Kurt high; they were simply stopping the sickness.

By the time they reached Paris on February 13, 1994, Kurt's typical melancholy mood turned darker. At a photo session, he insisted he be photographed with a gun in his mouth. It wasn't a real pistol, just a prop, but the gruesome humor no longer seemed remotely funny. It was the same shtick Kurt had been doing since he was a teenager—back in his first Super 8 films when he feigned suicide as a stunt. Considering how often he'd truly threatened to take his own life, and how many drug overdoses there had been, the photograph was the height of bad taste.

A week later, Kurt turned twenty-seven, and just a few days after that was his second wedding anniversary. Neither event was much celebrated on tour—Kurt planned to meet up with Courtney in Italy when the tour leg was over and to have a romantic reunion with her.

As the tour stretched on, Kurt repeatedly asked what might happen if they canceled the rest of their dates. He was told that there would be a huge financial consequence, and that promoters might sue the band if they didn't fulfill all the scheduled concerts. Already involved in the video lawsuit, Kurt wished to avoid more legal problems. On four previous tours, Kurt had managed to get Nirvana dates cut short when he complained of his health issues. Everyone reminded him that such behavior this time would immeasurably damage the band and hurt Kurt financially. While *In Utero* had started out as a fast seller, it was coming nowhere near the marks for *Nevermind*,

LEFT These "house rules" were originally posted on the refrigerator of the Cobains' Seattle house in 1993. The note to Courtney is from a friend in a Portland band. The name in the upper left is the Cobains' real estate agent, who helped them buy the mansion near Lake Washington in January 1994.

ABOVE Kurt and Frances, circa 1993.

selling at only about half the pace. Though Kurt had often told the press he didn't care about his sales, the album's failure to be a smash triggered his fears that his career might be short-lived.

The band arrived in Munich on March 1, 1994, for two shows in an abandoned airplane hangar. It was an awful venue for a concert—it was as cold as a freezer and had horrid acoustics. Nirvana didn't have much choice in venues in Europe since the classic opera houses wouldn't cater to them (because of the rowdiness of their audience), and outdoor arenas in winter were out of the question.

If things had been tense during the entire tour, they built to a crescendo in Munich. Two days earlier, Kurt had asked whether death would be a legitimate cause for cancellation of the rest of the tour. Before the show, Kurt had phoned Courtney, and they had argued, as was becoming increasingly common. Then, in a completely uncharacteristic move, Kurt called his fifty-two-year-old cousin Art Cobain back in Grays Harbor County. Kurt wasn't particularly close to Art, but he must have been desperate to talk to someone who had known him all his life. His cousin was delighted to hear from him, despite being woken from sleep by the phone call. "He really seemed to be reaching out," Art later told *People*. Kurt told him he was thinking of quitting the band and the music industry. Art invited Kurt to a Cobain family reunion that next summer.

The concert that night seemed doomed from the onset. The power went out after the sixth song and took several minutes to be restored. Kurt's voice was so hoarse it was little more than a croak. Nirvana ended the twenty-three-song set with "Heart-Shaped Box," and as Kurt left the stage, he headed directly to his agent. "That's it," Kurt said. "Cancel the next gig." It would be the last concert Nirvana would ever perform.

TWO DAYS LATER IN ROME, Kurt tried to kill himself. He and Courtney had reunited the previous evening, and after she fell asleep, he had mixed almost three dozen Rohypnol pills with champagne in what should have been a lethal dose. He had left a suicide note that quoted what the addiction doctor had told him that Christmas: "Like Hamlet," Kurt wrote, "I have to choose between life and death. I'm choosing death."

When Courtney awoke to find him, Kurt was rushed to the hospital, and several news reports prematurely announced he was dead. CNN ran a news bulletin on his obituary, as did a wire service. In one of the stranger incidents in a larger grisly story, an imposter phoned Nirvana's record company pretending to be label-head David Geffen. The fake Geffen announced that Kurt was dead and that everyone needed to be notified. Krist Novoselic, who had returned to Seattle during the break, received a phone call from a label representative telling him Kurt had died. It was several hours before the hoax was discovered.

ABOVE This hand-painted box was the last heart-shaped box Kurt ever gave to Courtney, in Rome in March 1994.

RIGHT A small sampling of the many travel documents and receipts that Kurt saved.

FOLLOWING Courtney cites this photograph as her single favorite picture of Kurt. It was taken at their North Seattle house in late 1993.

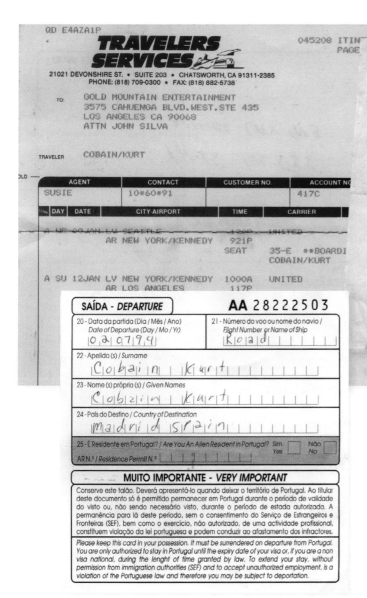

Though Kurt was in a coma for a day, he recovered quickly and, after a short hospital stay, headed back to Seattle. Some may have thought such a serious health crisis might scare Kurt, but even before he left Rome, he had called ahead to a dealer and arranged to have heroin waiting in the bushes outside his home. Compounding the issue, Kurt's management decided not to tell anyone that Rome was a suicide attempt and to stick with the "accidental overdose" story. Even Krist Novoselic—Kurt's bandmate for seven years—wasn't told it was a suicide attempt until later.

The end of Nirvana also represented a larger creative death for Kurt, who had always seen his band as a vital artistic outlet. Nirvana never even attempted anything as formal as a full-band rehearsal again, though Kurt did jam in his basement with Pat Smear and a few friends. By March 1994, Kurt had stopped thinking about any kind of future with the band, and he was no longer writing songs or planning another album. The band had meant so much to him for so many years, but when it fell apart, it caused him to retreat from his art across the board: He stopped painting, drawing, and working on his many collage projects. For so many years, his guitar or his paintbrush had helped him create an alternate universe, and they had given him wealth and fame beyond his dreams. But now it was only physical escape he sought, at the expense of everything else. Even his beloved collectibles were barely touched or toyed with, and the illustrated man and woman dolls grew dusty.

that the letter couldn't have been conceived by anyone on earth other than Kurt: "You won't miss my smelly crust or old man urine."

He closed the letter by restating what he had said four other times over the two pages: "I am officially stating on the record, for the last time, you're fired, Dave's fired, and I'm firing myself from this nightmare and starting over with others."

IN A WAY, WITH THE FULL-ON EMBRACE OF HIS ADDICTION, Kurt had chosen not only to quit Nirvana but to quit the rest of his life as well. When Courtney told him that he could no longer do drugs in their house, he simply left the home and checked in to cheap motels. His exit caused Courtney to panic, and she canceled his credit and bank cards, thinking that might put an end to his drug spree.

Rene Navarette was the only person with Kurt for much of the last week of March 1994. They were in an $18-a-night motel where the front desk also sold drugs. "It was like we were out on the town, without mom around," Navarette recalled. "We didn't have any money, so were having my

mom Western Union me, and I didn't have ID, so it had to be in Kurt's name." When they went to a Western Union office, one of the clerks remarked to Kurt, "What the fuck do you need $100 for?"

Navarette kept urging Kurt not to call Courtney, but Kurt kept dialing her from a pay phone, and each time a new argument would ensue. Despite the squalid motel room, Navarette thought Kurt didn't seem depressed but was simply resigned to the fact that he needed changes in his life. He talked about ending the band, getting divorced, and also trying a different music direction. "He was prepared to move on; it was scary and it made him feel really bad, but he had some definite ideas of what he was going to do with his money, his career, and his band," Navarette said. Like many of the conversations Kurt had that spring, it was impossible to know whether what he said was crazed drug talk, or whether it represented a rare moment of clarity in an increasingly opiate-addled mind.

Navarette recalled an earlier conversation where Kurt had talked wistfully about his time back in Olympia, when his creative powers were at an acme: "There was a lot that happened back then that inspired him, and he'd bring that up in reference to what it was like to have fun," Navarette said. "Nostalgically, he'd go back to that time. He did so much in such a short time." Kurt told Navarette that he thought it was hilarious that his favorite monkey, Chim-Chim, had ended up in the picture on the back cover of *Nevermind*. To Kurt, it seemed the ultimate irony: that this weird toy creation—as personal and as intimate as anything Kurt ever owned—had ended up on a CD that had sold over ten million copies. Chim-Chim had made the big time.

Kurt's lost week was interrupted only when Novoselic managed to guess where Kurt was staying and unexpectedly came to rescue him. "Krist said he had a bunch of instruments in the back of his car," Navarette recalled. "He said that he and Kurt could go off together, that he'd get Kurt a doctor, and that Kurt didn't need to go back to the house." Kurt, however, spurned the offer, jumped out of Krist's van, and headed for a drug dealer.

During the following week, two interventions were attempted, and neither went well. Patty Schemel was at one and saw how desperate and forlorn Kurt appeared: "Everyone was downstairs, and it was Pat Smear and I upstairs with Kurt. Kurt was more concerned with how he looked, and he didn't want everyone to see him as he was. He was putting on makeup, trying to clean up the bags under his eyes. He kept repeating, 'What am I going to do now?' He had that complete sense of being on the run. After that point, he was running. He just shut down to everything."

Kurt finally agreed to try another treatment program, and on March 30, 1994, he flew to Los Angeles and checked in to the Exodus Recovery Center. He stayed fewer than forty-eight hours before jumping over a wall to escape. His attempt at rehab seemed less than sincere when one considers the fact that on the day he flew down to Los Angeles, he had purchased a twenty-gauge

LEFT Kurt and Frances in Seattle, Christmas 1993.

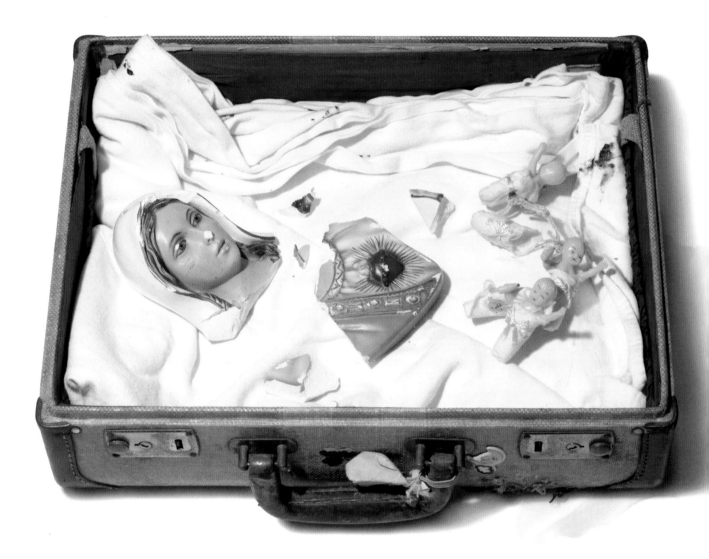

ABOVE Kurt was always fascinated by religious artifacts and collected many of them. In this thrift store suitcase, he arranged a collage of broken pieces of Madonna statuary with three birth-announcement dolls.

shotgun, which he had left in a secret compartment of his home closet. On the night of April 1, 1994, he caught a flight back to Seattle.

By chance, Duff McKagan of the band Guns N' Roses was on Kurt's plane. "He had just left rehab," McKagan recalled. "I knew from all my instinct that something was wrong, but I knew *I* wasn't going to die that day. I knew *I* wasn't going to go home and shoot up a bunch of heroin. I could tell he was bumming. You get that instinct from someone." McKagan offered Kurt a ride, but Kurt had a car service waiting for him.

Over the next three days, Kurt avoided his mansion and went missing again. He checked in to some of the same fleabag motels he'd favored in the past, but this time he was alone. "He was totally isolated," Navarette said, "and I think it was that isolation that did him in." Courtney was in Los Angeles going through rehab herself. She hired a private investigator to search for Kurt, though even Kurt's dealer didn't know where he was. A missing person's report was filed, but the police also failed to locate Kurt.

Eventually, Kurt slipped unnoticed back into his Lake Washington house, which was now empty of family. His toys and collectibles were all still in their boxes. His paintings and art projects were still crated up in the basement; in the three months he had lived in the house, most of his artwork had not made it onto the walls of the new home. Kurt's list of "house rules" was still stuck to the wall. "Petty, unnecessary waste and indulgence," he had written a few months before, a line that could have come straight out of "Smells Like Teen Spirit." Now, alone in his mansion, the last thing Kurt wrote was a suicide note.

Police would later find Kurt dead of a self-inflicted shotgun wound to the head, in his greenhouse. A half-empty can of Barq's Root Beer sat near him, and a small box with drug paraphernalia was also in the room. Next to his body was his final journal entry impaled on a pen stuck in a small potted plant.

The suicide note was addressed to Kurt's childhood imaginary friend, Boddah, who, like Chim-Chim, had been a constant companion wherever life had taken Kurt. In some small way, by addressing the note to Boddah, Kurt was letting everyone who knew him intimately—his original family, his closest friends, and his wife—know that this time he meant it. This was not like his other suicide attempts; it was different from his childhood desire to jump off a building or the many times he used enough drugs to blot out the pain forever.

In his last note, Kurt addressed the many frustrations he'd had with his career as well as the fact that he felt artistically bankrupt: "I haven't felt the excitement of listening to, as well as creating, music along with reading and writing for too many years now." Despite his best efforts, he couldn't get "over the frustration, the guilt and empathy I have for everyone." He was "too sensitive," he wrote, and that sensitivity made him "too fucking sad." He wrote that Courtney and Frances would be better off without him, and that he couldn't "stand the thought of his daughter becoming the miserable, self-destructive, death rocker that I've become." He ended by writing "peace, love, empathy," signing his name, and adding a postscript that said he loved his wife and child.

When police later examined the house, they found the television and stereo were still on. The television was tuned to MTV, though the sound was off. In the CD player was R.E.M.'s *Automatic for the People.*

THE LAST PRESS INTERVIEW KURT EVER GAVE was with Chuck Crisafulli for a Fender guitar publication. It was conducted by phone in the middle of February, and while Kurt didn't talk long, he sounded more sincere than he had in any other interview during that last year, with answers that were more insightful than usual. At times he appeared almost helpful, which itself was out of character when he was talking to the press. When asked if songwriting was part of his "job," he replied, "Writing is the one part that's not a job, it's expression." He called himself an "anti-guitar hero," complaining that he couldn't play as well as Segovia, but also joking that Segovia couldn't play like he did. It was a short interview, done to help promote a guitar that Kurt had designed for Fender called the "Jag-Stang." When asked what the biggest "drag" in his life was, Kurt said it was the long separations from his family. Crisafulli followed up by asking Kurt about his family, a topic that most journalists usually saved for last, just in case Kurt took offense at the personal inquiry and the interview ended prematurely. On this day though, Kurt seemed pleased to answer the question, as if it was the only thing he truly wanted to talk about. His family, he said, was "more important than anything else in the whole world. Playing music is what I do—my family is what I am."

There was a short pause, and then Kurt reflected on what his legacy ultimately might be, years after *In Utero* was no longer a current album and Nirvana wasn't at the top of the charts. This final interview was conducted on February 11, 1994, but what Kurt said mirrored some of the themes he'd touch on just two months later in his suicide note. "When everyone's forgotten about Nirvana, and I'm on some revival tour opening up for the Temptations and the Four Tops, Frances Bean will still be my daughter and Courtney will still be my wife. That means more than anything else to me."

As for the band, Kurt's comments were similar to those he addressed in his unsent letter to Krist Novoselic. "I'm extremely proud of what we've accomplished together," Kurt said. "Having said that, however, I don't know how long we can continue as Nirvana without a radical shift in direction. I have lots of ideas and musical ambitions that have nothing to do with this mass conception of 'grunge' that has been force-fed to the record-buying public these past few years." Kurt didn't outline those ideas, but he did say that he knew Krist and Dave also had musical ambitions that couldn't be met by the band.

The interview ran only ten minutes, and though even Kurt didn't know it would be his final talk with the press—he was in the middle of a tour, which often meant impromptu interviews—he sounded surprisingly serious, as if he wanted to set the record straight. Yet among Kurt's solemn replies to questions about the perils of stardom and the future of Nirvana, there was a hint of the same fellow who once lived in that smelly Olympia apartment. When asked about the trials of long tours, Kurt complained that the fancy caterers kept insisting on serving him "fine French meals," when what he truly wanted, and what his performance contract rider specifically called for, was pasta out of a box made by the second-largest food conglomerate in the world, Kraft. "All I want," he said in the last interview he ever gave, "is macaroni and cheese." ■

RIGHT Kurt Cobain, 1971.

ACKNOWLEDGMENTS

It was while working on *Heavier Than Heaven* in the late nineties that I first encountered Kurt Cobain's treasure trove of artwork and collectibles. As I interviewed Kurt's friends and family, they kept referring to the things Kurt collected with descriptions so diverse and grand that I thought they were exaggerating.

Eventually, I asked Courtney Love about Kurt's effects, and she told me that they were stored in a Seattle vault. All told, including Kurt's guitars and artwork, there were enough boxes to fill a U-Haul moving truck, a surprising amount of material considering that Kurt only had a permanent address for the last few years of his life. At the high-security storage facility, I had my retina scanned and was left alone with everything from old View-Master slides to priceless left-handed guitars. The material had been quickly stored in the days after Kurt's death in April 1994, and I was the first—and only person up to that point—to examine it. I was truly moved both by what Kurt had created and what he had collected.

When I initially brought up getting access to Kurt's things, Love not only gave me carte blanche permission, she did so without any restrictions, as long as I didn't photograph the items. It was much the same with his journals, and I specifically recall her telling me, "If you're going to write about Kurt, you'd better read what he wrote about himself." While I addressed this point in the acknowledgments of *Heavier Than Heaven,* I'm not sure I stressed enough that access was given without any strings: Love did not ask for, nor did she get, the ability to read my biography before publication. Rightly or wrongly, she trusted my ability to tell the story and sensed that only an independent biographer—one who would tell Kurt's story, and not mine or hers—was needed.

Cobain Unseen grew directly out of that initial conversation over a decade ago, and after my subsequent visits to the vault. Once I saw in the vault the bizarre and moving weirdness that represented the physical world of Kurt Cobain, I phoned Courtney and argued that if people were able to see Kurt's talent as a collector and artist, they might have a different understanding of how his creativity worked. Love eventually allowed Riverhead Books to publish a selection of Kurt's reproduced journal entries in 2002, though even the 400-some pages contained in that book were less than one-tenth of existing diary entries.

This book, however, is a peek inside what was in the vault, the visual and three-dimensional effects of Kurt Cobain, supplemented by other visuals that tell the same story. The explanations, analysis,

and captions here are my own—just like the disclaimer at the beginning of a DVD, you have only me to blame for anything expressed, whether brilliant or blockheaded. Still, obviously this book would not have been possible without the trust accorded to me by the Estate of Kurt Cobain, Love, and the various friends and family who loaned items for this book.

No individual helped shape the actual book more than Ava Stander, whose appreciation of clean design, great music, and London punk rock clubs is unsurpassed. Marie Walsh Dixon (a true goddess) was also essential, as was photographer Geoff Moore, who took many of the marvelous shots of these objects. My agent, Sarah Lazin, followed this project from inception to completion, over years. Also, special thanks to Ava's mother, Maria Penn, for her unlimited patience.

The crew at becker&mayer!, particularly Meghan Cleary, was also indispensable in seeing this crazy idea take shape into an even crazier book. I'd also like to thank Andy Mayer, Shayna Ian, Joanna Price, and Leah Finger. At Little, Brown and Co., Michael Sand committed to this project early on, while Michael Pietsch has encouraged my work since my first book twenty years ago.

Other thanks are due to my many interview subjects and the many photographers who contributed. I also want to specifically thank Ryan Aigner, Joris Baas, Earnie Bailey, Janet Billig, Peter Blecha, Mari Earl, the Experience Music Project, Erik Flannigan, Tony Frick, JJ Gonson, Joe Guppy, Rasmus Holmen, John Keister, Michael Lavine, Geoff MacPherson, Tracy Marander, Jacob McMurray, Carl Miller, Shawn Mitchell, Rene Navarette, Charles Peterson, Larry Schemel, Patty Schemel, Neal Skok, Matt Smith, Jaan Uhelszki, and Alice Wheeler.

Finally, I'd like to acknowledge my family—Ashland and Katharine—for their support, love, and eternal patience during many late nights and a few very early mornings. The oatmeal, the coffee, the mash notes, and the crayon drawings—perhaps one day to be memorialized in their own book—are all more appreciated than I ever said.

ABOVE The author's backstage pass to Nirvana's December 13, 1993, show, one of their last performances in Seattle.

—**CHARLES R. CROSS**
Seattle, Washington, April 2008

ABOUT THE AUTHOR

CHARLES R. CROSS was editor of *The Rocket*, the Northwest music magazine, from 1985 through 2000. *The Rocket* ran the first ever cover story on Nirvana, and it was where the band often turned to advertise for drummers. Cross is the author of five other books including *Room Full of Mirrors: A Biography of Jimi Hendrix* and *Led Zeppelin: Heaven and Hell*. He also authored *Heavier Than Heaven: A Biography of Kurt Cobain*, which won the ASCAP Timothy White Award for Outstanding Biography. Cross writes for numerous newspapers and magazines on music, pop culture, and parenting. He lives near Seattle with his family. You can find him on the Web at www.charlesrcross.com.

ABOVE The April 13 issue of *The Rocket* was originally scheduled with a cover story on Hole's album *Live Through This*. When the news broke on April 8 that Kurt had been found dead, Courtney was taken off the cover in favor of this Charles Peterson image of Kurt performing at the Motor Sports International Garage show. The issue hit stands just a few days after the news of Kurt's death. For Northwest readers, who had followed the chronicle of Nirvana from their rise, no headline was needed.

PAGE 160 Kurt initially wanted this heart-shaped box to be pictured on the cover for *In Utero*. The many parts to this album cover were some of his last visual creations.

IMAGE CREDITS

Every effort has been made to trace copyright holders. If any unintended omissions have been made, becker&mayer! would be pleased to add appropriate acknowledgement in future editions.

All photographs, illustrations, documents, and removable facsimiles are courtesy of the Estate of Kurt Cobain, except as noted: Endsheet maps: Courtesy of John Kirkwood/Grays Harbor County Department of Public Services; Page 23: Experience Music Project; Page 28 (both): Photos by Ryan Sutherby; Page 30-31 (drawings): Collection of Joris Baas; Page 35: Photo by Alice Wheeler; Page 36 (top): Photo by Tracy Marander; Page 38 (outside flap, both): Photos by Tracy Marander; Page 41 (all): Photos by Tracy Marander; Page 42: Photo by Tracy Marander; Page 45: Photo by Alice Wheeler; Page 47 (contact sheet): Photos by Charles Peterson; Page 48 (top and center): Photos by JJ Gonson; Page 51 (top): Photo by JJ Gonson; Page 54: © Steve Double/Retna Ltd.; Page 55 (bottom): Photo by Charles Peterson; Page 57: © Michael Lavine; Page 60: © Ian Tilton; Page 62 (outside flap, lyrics): "Smells Like Teen Spirit," Words and Music by Kurt Cobain, Krist Novoselic and Dave Grohl, © 1991 THE END OF MUSIC, PRIMARY WAVE TUNES, M.J. TWELVE MUSIC and MURKY SLOUGH MUSIC. All Rights for THE END OF MUSIC and PRIMARY WAVE TUNES Controlled and Administered by EMI VIRGIN SONGS, INC. All Rights for M.J. TWELVE MUSIC Controlled and Administered by SONGS OF UNIVERSAL, INC. All Rights Reserved. International Copyright Secured. Used by Permission.; Page 66: Photo by Alice Wheeler; Page 67: © Ian Tilton; Page 69: © Michael Lavine; Page 70: © Blecken/Sunshine/Retna Ltd.; Page 71: Photo by Todd Bates; Page 77: © Joe Giron/Corbis; Page 81: © James Rexroad; Page 82 (top): Photo by Darrell M. Westmoreland (www.dmwimages.com); Page 87 (hinged card): The Sub Pop logo is provided courtesy of Sub Pop Records. Sub Pop is a registered trademark of Sub Pop Records.; Page 104: © Mark Seliger/Contour by Getty Images; Page 106: Courtesy of Spin Magazine, cover photograph by Guzman; Page 107 (bottom right): © Stephen Sweet/Retna Ltd.; Page 122 (outside and inside flap): Photos by Charles Peterson; Page 127 (painting): © 1992 by The Williams S. Burroughs Trust, reprinted with the permission of The Wylie Agency, Inc.; Page 129: Photo by David Sims; Page 130: Photo by Charlie Hoselton; Page 133: Photo by Charles Peterson; Page 134 (both): © Kevin Mazur/WireImage; Page 136: Photo by Alice Wheeler; Page 137: © Kevin Mazur/WireImage; Page 138 (both): © Frank Micelotta/Getty Images; Page 139: Courtesy of Michael Stipe; Page 141: © Kevin Mazur/WireImage; Page 148 (outside flap): © Mark Seliger/Contour by Getty Images; Page 149: Photo by Patty Schemel; Page 157: Courtesy of Charles R. Cross; Page 158 (author photo): Photo by Rick Dahms; Page 158 (The Rocket): Courtesy of Charles R. Cross

The photographs on pages 1, 8, 24-25, 40, 43 (binder), 49, 53, 62 (journals), 72 (box), 75 (sneakers), 78 (all), 95 (doll head and guitar), 97, 98-99, 100 (outside flap), 102, 103, 116-117, 124-125 (heart-shaped boxes), 144, 152, and 160 were taken at OTMFC Studios on October 4, 2007, and are credited as follows: Photography: Geoff Moore (www.geoffmoorestudio.com); Lighting Director: Keith Leman; Digital Technician: Daniel Goldwasser

Image scans and restoration for the Cobain Estate archives: Bonny Diadhiou of the Icon photography lab

Page 116 (CD Track1): © 2008 Charles R. Cross

Page 116 (CD Track2): © 2008 The End of Music LLC; digital transfer: Martyn Le Noble

"THE BRIDGE"

ABERDEEN
1970 Population 18,489
1979 Estimate 19,075

WEATHERWAX
HIGH SCHOOL

COBAINS
1210 E. FIRST
KURT 1968-1986

"THINK OF ME"
HILL